To Car

IN THE SHADOW
OF SHAKESPEARE

© RICHARD VAUGHAN DAVIES

**DEDICATED TO THE MEMORY OF
WILLIAM SHAKE-SPEARE**

The greatest writer the world has ever known

In memory of my dear friend and mentor Cyril Davies, who first sparked my interest in the story of Shakespeare's life.

To all the hard-working members of the tourist trade and the theatres of Stratford-upon-Avon, who have given such pleasure to over three million visitors to the town each year, all inspired by the genius of William Shakespeare. They are presently dealing with very difficult circumstances.

All the quotations are from
The Tragical History of Hamlet, Prince of Denmark
by **William Shake-speare** (sic)
(published in 1603)

or from

Shake-speare's *Sonnets* (sic)
(published in 1609)

NOTE TO THE READER

No prior knowledge of Shakespeare or his work is necessary for the enjoyment of this story. However it may be helpful to know that at the back of the book you can find a summary of the plot of "Hamlet", timelines of the lives of William Shaxpur and Edward de Vere, a list of relevant books, and the text of some of the Sonnets.

Who's there? Stand and unfold yourself!
HAMLET Act 1, scene i, line 1

1

The actors are come hither, my Lord
Act 2, scene ii

"*Soft you now! The fair Ophelia. Nymph, in thy orisons be all my sins remembered!*"

The mellifluous voice with its richly modulated tones rang out across the rehearsal room, and the small audience of actors and technicians watched in silence as Ophelia faced Hamlet.

"*I did love you once.*" Hamlet's voice was mocking and his pleasure from taunting her apparent. Ophelia looked up at him, distressed by her Lord's manner, fear and adoration mixed in her gaze.

"*Indeed, my Lord, you made me believe so.*"

"*You should not have believed me! I loved you not.*"

Ophelia winced as if she had received a slap in the face, then responded quietly.

"*I was the more deceived.*"

Now Hamlet sprang threateningly towards her, screaming.

"*Get thee to a nunnery! Why wouldst thou be a breeder of sinners? Farewell.*"

Ophelia crumpled before their eyes, a beautiful puppet doll whose strings had been cut. Only her tormentor's grip on her shoulders prevented her from falling. Hamlet held her at arm's length, a specimen to be examined.

Hamish realised he was literally gritting his teeth, and he averted his eyes from the stage. Olivia was so moving in the part that watching her being ill-treated made him feel physically sick. Certainly it was hot in the rehearsal room, and the atmosphere was oppressive, but watching Olivia acting moved him. She had a subtlety and sweetness that melted the heart, as she magically transformed herself into the hapless Ophelia.

Today Hamish could even believe that she really was in love with her Lord, and he shook his head crossly at the thought. He twisted around on his plastic seat, which had clearly been designed by someone totally ignorant of the human anatomy, and wriggled to stop it digging into his back.

The Royal Shakespeare Theatre's rehearsal stage held just two figures. Ophelia was the picture of young beauty, brave but vulnerable. Prince Hamlet was tall and slim, his short blond hair contrasting with his black Lycra suit and black trainers. From the thousand-seater main auditorium, he would look young and handsome, but Hamish was sitting close enough to see beneath the makeup covering the lines and pitted skin of a much older man.

"To a nunnery, go, and quickly too! Farewell!"

The Prince was still railing at Ophelia. Olivia's face dissolved, and tears were clearly not far away.

"Heavenly powers, restore him."

But a sharp voice cut in on the action.

"All right! Thanks, Ol, you can save your tears for now." The director was sitting cross-legged on a cushion on the steps to the side of the stage, a sharp-featured young woman with closecropped hair. Her unsmiling face bore no traces of make-up. The cast had nicknamed her Griselda and made jokes about a broomstick and a cat, though not to her face.

She tapped her fingers on her notebook and addressed the Sir.

"We'll go back to the beginning of that scene again, just after your soliloquy. I'll spare you '*To be or not to be*' for now. You and I can go over that later. Take it from '*Soft you now, the fair Ophelia*', will you? Tone it down a couple of decibels, and move a little further upstage."

The Sir opened his mouth as if to protest, then closed it again.

"Ol, mind that gesture on '*I loved you not*'. You've used it before, and it needs to be fresh. Oh, and while I think of it, Steve, that dimmer light..." She turned to the lighting technician and they put their heads together as the actors waited on the stage.

The man with the grey beard sitting next to Hamish turned to whisper to him, fumbling in his Elizabethan doublet for his cigarettes and lighter.

"I think this is my moment to get some fresh air. Fancy joining me for a smoke outside?"

Hamish smiled to think of Polonius being a cigarette smoker. He nodded and stood up.

"Good idea, Polly. Yes, I'll come and keep you company."

"It's a treat watching Olivia in the part. She's just magic. More than I can say about the Sir though..." Polly shook his head. "Must be hard for you having to watch him mangle the part. Makes me thankful my understudy days are long over."

"Don't know about that, Polly. But you're right, I've had about as much of this as I can stand... How's it going with you?"

The older man stopped at the doorway.

"All right, I suppose. I can think of better ways of spending a sunny day than poncing around in here with this lot though. Don't tell me, I've been doing this job too long. But at least I don't have to act with that slimy popinjay breathing in my face. God, his breath smells like rotting fish. Poor little Ol."

Hamish enjoyed talking to Polly, especially about his days working with the great and the dead.

"I don't think he gets much pleasure from the love scenes, in all fairness. Probably a huge effort for him, given that Ol's so much a woman."

He glanced across the room, where Olivia was in deep conversation with Griselda. When Hamish caught her eye she smiled and raised a hand in acknowledgement as the two men left.

2

Marry, this is miching maleccho. It means mischief
Act III, scene ii

They cut through the maze of corridors and emerged blinking into the sunlight, stepping onto the terrace at the back of the Royal Shakespeare Theatre complex. Several people were chatting, many gazing at the river.

Hamish's eye was caught by a famous face at one table, talking earnestly to a stout man in a suit. The etiquette was to be cool and not stare, but he loved to see a celebrity. Childish, he knew, but it still thrilled him. It was the magic of theatre.

The celebrity was saying in a low but penetrating voice, "Just as long as it's clearly understood."

"We've been through this already. It's a no brainer. How many more times?"

"*Above* the title, all right? Sorry to be boring, dear heart, but I've learnt the hard way. We need to get these things clear at the outset."

A couple close enough to overhear the conversation were grinning. The reply from the other man was inaudible.

"Not that it matters to me personally, of course. I'm past that sort of pettiness, thank the Lord. But, as you of all people are aware, it matters to those who care about these

5

things. And they pay my salary and yours."

There was no reply. Polly had his back to them and raised his eyebrows to Hamish as if asking for a commentary.

"The face is waiting for a response," whispered Hamish. "It has ostentatiously wiped its mouth with a napkin and sat back in its chair. The suit has merely shrugged and is flicking through its mobile. Now it's whispering something to the face. Oh wait - they're getting up and going."

"Show's over then," said Polly.

Hamish leant forward.

"Did you get all that?" he said. "That must be his agent he's talking to. He's got a big part coming up. Movie? Telly?"

Polly laughed aloud.

"Oh, come on, Ham," he said. "I don't think so. Can't you spot a setup when you see one? His career's been on the blink for years. So he's showing his face in Stratford, to get himself talked about again. Nice try. It might even work."

After a moment, Hamish laughed too. The two friends turned to watching the river scene. Swans mingled with Canada geese in the packed water, seemingly indifferent to their presence. Pairs of delicately coloured mallards moved in between the bigger birds like fishing boats dodging cross-Channel ferries in a crowded shipping lane.

Polly drew on his cigarette and turned to Hamish.

"Talking of setups, what about old Shaxpur then? Have you learnt much about him?"

"Who?" said Hamish.

"William Shaxpur of course, to give him the name on his wedding entry. The guy from Stratford who couldn't decide how to spell his own name. The man whose father and his two daughters were illiterate. Who had no education that we know of, and at his death left his wife his second-best bed but no books, notes, or letters."

"He was a bit more than that though, wasn't he?" said Hamish, amused. "I think genius is the word you're looking for."

"Go on, Polly. Tell him," said a voice. They looked up.

"Oh, hi Oz. Didn't see you inside."

"No, Griselda's not doing my scenes till later. Poor Osric is feeling a bit left out, darlings."

Oz had come up to join them, unnoticed. His dark skin glistened in the sunshine, and he made a handsome picture in his colourful courtier's costume. The style suited him, and he knew it.

"Can I cadge a ciggie off you, darling?"

"Of course. And, if you listen you might learn something," said Polly. "Just telling Ham about Shaxpur. Did you know that in the Bard's lifetime, he wasn't known as a playwright or writer of any sort in Stratford? Just as a businessman. Nor is Stratford ever mentioned in his plays. His famous tomb wasn't erected until several years after he died, and even now it bears no name. Just saying…"

Hamish scratched his jaw.

"I've heard this sort of thing before, and that the whole tomb thing looks very contrived. But so what? It doesn't mean Shakespeare didn't write Shakespeare, does it?"

"Not necessarily, I suppose, " said Polly, "But some say that Will Shaxpur, the local boy who never went to university or travelled, couldn't conceivably have written the Bard's works. The writer's knowledge of philosophy, classical literature, history and courtly life was unparalleled. He must have been steeped in learning from a very early age."

Hamish shrugged.

"So, he read up on it all. What does that prove? That a country boy from Warwickshire couldn't have studied history and law?"

"Of course not. But there's not a scrap of documentary evidence for it. The fact remains that, apart from his acting career in London, the man from Stratford had no claims to being a writer whatsoever. He didn't even leave a book or a document in his will."

"You know what?" said Oz. "I've always found this intriguing. As a matter of fact, the sonnets interest me more than the plays in this connection. That's where the Bard shows his true inner thoughts." He screwed up his face. "I might look into it a bit more, you know. It'll give me something to do. God knows, I've got enough time on my hands -- Osric only has twenty-five lines in the whole play, and one of them is *Sir*!"

"You're lucky," said Hamish. "Hamlet has fourteen hundred lines to say. I've had to learn every one of them, but as an understudy I never get to say a word!"

The others laughed, and Polly straightened up from the terrace wall.

"There is a real mystery here, whether you like it or not. They say that if Shaxpur were suddenly proposed now out of the blue as the playwright, purely on the grounds that his name was similar to the name on the later plays, the idea would be laughed out of court. A businessman with no record of any study or travel or education, who left no trace of having any literary connections whatsoever, being the greatest genius the world has ever known? A vast knowledge of philosophy, history, courtly life, the classics, possibly more than any other man before him, showing no evidence of existing in his life at all? Utterly preposterous. The idea is inconceivable."

He threw his cigarette into the river, and watched it fall where the mallards and moorhens were scrabbling for bread. Two green-headed ducks rushed up to snap eagerly at the butt, but turned away unimpressed.

"Yet because of an unconvincing tomb and some weird inscriptions appearing in the church down there after he had been dead for several years, and Jonson's remark about 'Sweet Swan of Avon', this enormous Shakespearean legend has built up. Beyond amazing, you must admit."

Hamish said nothing. For some reason a tingle ran down his spine. His mind began racing. Polly looked at him thoughtfully.

"Tell you what," he said. "If you're at all interested, why don't you both come and have supper at my place one evening next week? Do some research before you come, and I'll tell you a bit more. You might actually learn something. Bring Olivia with you, Ham." He paused. "I could do my signature dish. *Canard a l'orange,* plus a secret ingredient. I know! I'll nick one of those ducks from the river – when all the tourists have gone, of course – and pop him in a pot."

Polly leant over the wall and pointed a finger at a handsome duck on the footpath. It stared back defiantly. Oz called down, "You'd better look out, ducky! He's got his eye on you, with some asparagus and Jersey Royals. Yum yum!"

The duck quacked and waddled off indignantly.

Hamish grinned. "All right, Polly, that sounds good. You can reveal the darkest secret of Shakespeare's true identity and ruin our illusions forever. Can't see Ol standing for that, by the way. She won't want her dreams trodden on, I warn you now."

"I hear where you're coming from," said Polly. "But stand by for some startling revelations. Now, back to the grindstone."

He moved towards the theatre, and the others followed slowly. Oz spoke quietly to Hamish.

"What do you reckon about Will not being the Bard? Something in it, do you think?"

Hamish hesitated. "Well, I understand the guy didn't get much recognition when he was alive. But there is something about the whole thing that doesn't add up, that seems obvious. I'd like to know more about it, I must say. Let's say I'm intrigued." With that, he and Oz followed Polly back into the theatre.

As soon as she saw them come in, Olivia left the side of the stage and came over towards Hamish, taking his hand.

"This is a nightmare. Griselda can't stop fine tuning. You wouldn't think the play was already up and running. I'm actually on tonight again. Can't wait for our day off tomorrow when we do our tourist thing."

Hamish squeezed her hand in encouragement. "Me too. Maybe we'll find out a few home truths about Master Will. Looking forward to it."

Olivia frowned at Hamish in puzzlement. But before he could expand, a rap on Griselda's notebook called the actors to order.

Hamish resumed his place as a spectator. He tried to

concentrate on the play, but his mind was buzzing. He had a strange feeling of excitement. Something was stirring inside him, hard to define. It was a feeling that vanished as soon as he tried to grasp it, as a dream dies at the waking day. He shook his head and concentrated on the play.

They were doing the scene where Rosencrantz and Guildenstern had unexpectedly arrived at the palace. Now if he were doing the part, Hamish thought, he would turn his back on the audience at this point. All that would be seen would be his hands twisting together to show his doubt at the visitors' motives. But the Sir had begun to shout again. Hamish sighed.

3

Costly thy habit as thy purse can buy
But not expressed in fancy; rich, not gaudy
Act I, scene iii

"Knock, knock!"

"Oh no you don't! Get off me! We're just going into town!" cried Olivia, struggling to get out of Hamish's grasp. But he had seized her from behind and pushed her over the end of the sofa, and she couldn't escape. "And mind the coffee cups! It's not our carpet you know."

"Knock, knock!"

"Oh, all right then," she gasped. "Who's there?"

"Ophelia."

Olivia couldn't stop herself giggling.

"Ophelia who?"

"Ophelia finest features!"

"Just get your hands off them!"

"And very fine they are, too."

Hamish grinned as he pushed his hair off his forehead with the back of his hand. He was looking too pleased with himself, Olivia thought. In a flash she had reversed the roles and grabbed him by the shoulders. She shoved his head down into the big leather cushion on the sofa.

"Knock, knock!" she squealed.

"Who's there?" Hamish's voice was muffled by the cushion.

"*Hamlet,*" said Olivia, squeezing his neck from behind.

He winced.

"*Ow*! Okay, Hamlet, who?"

"Ham lettin' you get away with that, just this once, but don't you dare try it again!"

She released her grasp on his neck and they both lay back on the sofa, engulfed in each other's limbs, hooting with laughter. She found herself running a thoughtful finger down his neck and pulled back abruptly.

"That *Knock knock* worked rather well, didn't it?" murmured Hamish. "I say, Ol, that weed last night must have been pretty powerful. Tell you what – shall we have another drag before we go out?"

Olivia let out a sigh and sat up, tugging her pink T-shirt down towards her gym-toned stomach. Was it a bit too tight across the chest? So little material, such a lot of money for just a silly label. She jumped up, pushing Hamish away.

"Not now. Look at that sun outside! This is our first real morning off since we came to Stratford. We're going to do a tour of the town, home of the Bard, our sole inspiration, remember? *Your doublet's all ungyved, Lord Hamlet* – do yourself up. And have you got your scarf?"

"Of course," said Hamish, still panting. "An actor without his scarf? You know perfectly well it means instant dismissal from Equity for an *act-or* to be seen in public without his casually knotted scarf."

Olivia laughed again, knowing the truth of this.

"You're right, let's go and explore. Hamish nodded in agreement. "Where do you want to go first?"

"Oh, the Birthplace, I think," said Olivia. "It's only round the corner from here, isn't it? Then to New Place in Chapel Street before lunch. Okay with that? Right, I'm just popping into the bathroom to freshen up. Won't be a tick."

"You decide where," said Hamish. "I'll leave it to you. It's ridiculous that it's taken us all this time to do the tourist thing."

He pushed his shirt back into his trousers and stretched his arms. Time he went back to the theatre gym. He had missed a couple of days lately, and his body knew it. He grimaced.

In the bathroom, Olivia had a moment to reflect, checking her face in the mirror. Today, Griselda had relented and given the whole cast a morning off. Let's make the most of it, Olivia thought. She put the lipstick away and gave her hair another quick brush.

"Right, I'm ready." She glanced down at her legs, twisting her head round. Hamish hugged her and gave her a smacking kiss. "Come on, let's go."

A minute later, they were out on the sun-drenched streets of Stratford-upon-Avon, busy with tourists and shoppers. Everywhere were roses and primulas neatly laid out in the municipal flowerbeds, and stalls selling souvenirs and snacks outside the theatre. Street acts were showing off their skills on the grass behind, with some of the performers in Elizabethan costume. The carnival atmosphere was infectious.

"Isn't it just amazing to be walking the same streets as Shakespeare did, watching the swans on the same river, drinking in pubs that he would have known?" said Olivia, taking Hamish's arm and chattering excitedly. "Shakespeare, not the swans, I mean. I almost can't believe it, can you?"

"I know," said Hamish, biting into a strawberry-flavoured ice cream he had just bought. "Do you want a lick? Come on! I wonder what he'd think of it today. This billion-pound tourist industry, all these happy people, all in his name, this amazing Shakespeare industry – wouldn't he have been so proud?"

They were walking past a bus stop where a crowd of chattering visitors were alighting from a coach that bore the name of a Yorkshire tour company. As they passed, two elderly women were climbing carefully down the steps of the bus. One said to the other, a worried expression on her face, "The trouble is, I don't really like Shakespeare, tha knows."

Her friend replied, "No, I know, lass, but never mind. There are some *reet* good shoe shops in Stratford."

This overheard exchange made Olivia and Hamish giggle. "If we thespians ever need to look for a proper job…" Hamish managed to say, "…there are some *reet* good shoe shops in Stratford."

This set them off again.

4

**But you must know your father lost a father,
That father lost, lost his.**
Act I, scene ii

Very soon, they arrived in Henley Street, where they presented their passes at the
  ticket office in entrance to the lovely half-timbered brick building proudly labelled 'Shakespeare's Birthplace'. They joined a group of Korean visitors to follow an older man guiding them around the house. Hamish whispered in Olivia's ear, "Why are they all wearing glasses?"

"Because they're all very intelligent," she whispered back.

The guide heard them and smiled in agreement.

They drifted along with the others. Hamish became aware that he and Olivia made a handsome couple, young, confident and attractive. He smoothed his hair back and straightened his shoulders, conscious of their fellow tourists looking at them. Was it respect, perhaps even awe, that he detected in their glances as they passed through the house? Either way it was a pleasant feeling.

"William Shakespeare was born and brought up in this house," intoned the guide. "It was the home of his parents, John and Mary. The house doubled as a workshop for his father's glove making business. After his father's death,

William inherited the property and part of it became an inn. It was purchased by the Shakespeare Birthplace Trust in 1847 and considerably restored…"

The old man coughed. He had a pleasant, scholarly face. He wore horn-rimmed glasses on a cord round his neck, and a battered tweed jacket. Olivia imagined she could smell pipe tobacco. He reminded her of Mr Kennedy, her history teacher at school.

"Now, this bedroom here may be the very room Shakespeare was born in." The guide indicated it proudly.

Hamish and Olivia gazed at the bedroom, with its simple oak furniture and basic personal accessories. They shook their heads in wonderment, and Olivia silently squeezed Hamish's hand. The other visitors were listening intently to the guide.

"From the mid 1580s onwards, Will started to divide his life between London and Stratford as his career developed, working both as an actor in London and writing his plays. In 1594, he bought shares in the theatrical company known as The Lord Chamberlain's Men. And by 1597 he was so successful that he could leave London and purchase what would become the finest house in Stratford, now called New Place, when he was only 33 years old."

Olivia whispered to Hamish that they would go to New Place next.

"He began purchasing more land and property, and by the turn of the century he was one of the richest men in the town. Incidentally there are over 70 written records of his transactions in the archives."

"When did he marry Anne Hathaway?" asked one of the

Korean tourists, a serious-faced young man, peering over his glasses at the guide. "How many children did they have?"

"They married in 1582 and had three children, one of whom, Hamnet, died when he was eleven. That must have been a terrible event for the young couple."

Personal grief being a tragedy that transcends time and setting, the listeners all nodded in sympathy. They began filing out of the bedroom in awed silence.

Hamish and Olivia ducked under heavy twisted wooden beams and followed the other visitors down the creaking wooden backstairs, out to the well-maintained gardens in the sunshine. The tourists had moved on to the gift shop, talking animatedly, and clearly thrilled with their experience. The guide, who had stayed behind, smiled encouragingly at the couple.

"Can you tell us something about the whole thing?" Hamish asked. "We're from the theatre, but we haven't even had time to read a travel guide. How did Shakespeare divide his time between here and London, for instance? It was a long way to travel, wasn't it? How did they do it then?"

"And what about Anne Hathaway, and the children?" Olivia chipped in. "Where did they live? Is it true he dumped Anne? Surely not?"

Hamish grinned at her enthusiasm and put an arm round her waist. She looked lovely in the sun, he thought. She was a sunshine girl, fair and tanned.

It was much quieter in the garden now. The guide seemed ready to chat while keeping half an eye on the house. He handed the couple a leaflet.

"I can't answer all your questions, but I'll do what I can.

Yes, we think he lived mostly here, but travelled up and down to London to oversee the production of his plays." He coughed. "The pieces of evidence about William Shakespeare are mostly legal documents, concerned with property and such matters. He was very prosperous and no mean businessman. He was also quite litigious, it has to be said! Matters like boundary disputes, late payment of taxes, arguments with neighbours... many documents of that nature. Nothing literary to tickle our palates, I'm afraid!"

"But he had time to write all those plays as well. Wow! A genius indeed," said Hamish, shaking his head in admiration. Olivia thought she detected a note of cynicism in his voice, and frowned at him, puzzled. Behind them a crowd of schoolchildren burst into the gardens, while a teacher in a tracksuit imparted a stream of information at the top of her voice. Few of the children seemed to pay her much attention but giggled amongst themselves or stared into their phones.

"Come on, Ham, this gentleman has enough to do without us taking up his time. Thank you so much. Fascinating stuff!" Olivia took Hamish's hand and firmly led him away. "Onto the next place!"

"But I'm just getting interested in all this... I need more detail."

"Plenty of time to learn more," cried Olivia.

5

They meandered down to the High Street, stopping to look in W H Smith's windows at the theatrical books' display, and then along Church Street to New Place. Everywhere, the shops were busy and the locals mixed with the crowds of tourists from various countries. The balmy air was a babble of different languages, all expressing the excitement of being in the birthplace and home of the greatest writer the world has ever known.

They walked past a restaurant called The Food of Love, and the Bard's Walk precinct, and smiled. A pub was advertising Shakesbeer and Shakeyburgers, illustrated as usual by the standard portrait of the Bard, with his high bald forehead and his ruff. A cab proclaiming 'Othello Taxis' was disgorging tourists by the kerbside.

At New Place, of which today only the garden still exists, they were shown round Nash's House, a beautifully restored Elizabethan house, furnished in contemporary style. At an oak writing desk they were invited to take a seat in the great man's chair, where it was stated his work may have been done. They were told *The Tempest* might have been created on this very spot.

Olivia felt dizzy with pleasure and found herself clutching Hamish's hand. He smiled, and felt moved. But all he said was, "That was interesting. I'll be ready for a pint after this."

A few minutes later, they slipped away. Nearby stood the ancient half-timbered King Edward VI school, proudly proclaiming '*The poet and playwright William Shakespeare attended this school in the 1570s*'. It was on the corner of a lane which led them to the riverside, past the garden of New Place. Walking down the lane, they were soon opposite the Royal Shakespeare Theatre, the older Swan Theatre beside it.

The famous pub the Dirty Duck, previously known as The Black Swan and frequented by generations of actors and playgoers, was nearby. The prospect of a drink and some congenial company lured them towards it.

Olivia managed to get two seats outside on the patio under the ancient mulberry tree, while Hamish went inside the pub to get a pint of Hooky and a glass of wine. As he waited to be served in the crowded bar, he looked as he always did at the faded photographs on the pub walls of the great stars of the past who had drunk there. Olivier, Gielgud, Ashcroft, Stephens and Redgrave looked haughtily back at him as if challenging him to emulate them. The portraits of the new giants of the stage, Rylance, Jacobi, McKellen, Dench, Branagh, were there too, though altogether friendlier and more casual.

"Mind where you're sitting," warned Olivia, when he returned to the patio. "These berries are lethal for staining your clothes."

"I know," said Hamish irritably. "You tell me that every time we come here." They sipped their drinks contentedly together, looking across the lane towards the busy river, which was crowded with people enjoying the sunshine. "You know, we are just so lucky to be here," said Olivia dreamily. "It's a fantasy come true. And we're actually performing *Hamlet* in the place where it may have been written. Just think, Shakespeare may have sat in this very pub, scribbling. Pure magic."

They sat in silence for a while with the sun warming their faces.

"Oh look! There's Oz!" Olivia cried. "*Ozzie!* Hi! Come and join us!"

Up the little steps from the lane to the garden came their fellow actor, the personification of his part in Hamlet as Osric, the gay courtier. He looked across and waved. His normally serious face broke into a grin when he saw Hamish and Olivia. He did a mime from the pub door which said, "I'll just get myself a drink, then I'll join you."

He soon reappeared with a glass of fruit juice and perched precariously beside them on the wooden bench that was built around the ancient tree.

"Well, what have you two lovebirds been doing with your morning off? Or shouldn't I ask?"

"Ozzie! Really! As if! Whatever are you suggesting?" said Olivia with a mock pout, rolling her eyes seductively and patting her hair. "I really don't know how you can say these terrible things to a *lay-dee*."

"Matter of fact," said Hamish, taking a long pull of his pint of ale, "we've been indulging in a bit of culture! We've been to the Bard's birthplace, and where his posh house used to be, and now we're fully *au fait* with all his life here in Stratters. Mm, this beer is de-li-cious."

"Hang on! We haven't finished with the Bard yet," said Olivia. "Next time that little madam gives us any time off, we're going to see Shakespeare's tomb and his memorial and the place where he is buried and a few other things. Aren't we, darling? Isn't it exciting?"

"Aha! Maybe you'll find out a bit more about Polly's theory, then? Did you tell Ol about his bombshell? I must say, it gave me something to think about. How about you, Ham?"

"What's all this?" asked Olivia. "It's all news to me. What theory?"

Hamish was spared from having to find an explanation by a voice breaking in on their conversation.

"Excuse us interrupting. May we just say hello?"

They all looked up. A middle-aged couple at the next table had stood up and were moving towards them. They had been observing the little group for some time, but they could obviously contain themselves no longer.

"We saw the play last night. It was wonderful. You are Ophelia, aren't you? And we've seen you on tv in that…"

"Yes," said Olivia, smiling at them. "In that awful soap about the motorway service station. How sweet of you to remember."

"You're the perfect choice for Ophelia," said the woman, "especially when you go mad. But we always wonder – how on earth do you learn all those lines?"

"And you were in it too!" said the man to Oz, fortunately saving Olivia from producing her stock answer to this question. "You really stood out in that scene at the end."

"Did I? Is it coz I is black?" asked Oz innocently, using

a television comedian's current catchphrase. Olivia kicked him on the ankle beneath the bench. The man flushed and started to stammer a reply. His wife saved him by turning quickly to Hamish, who was staring across at the river trying to be invisible. The Canada geese suddenly took off in a noisy crowd, swooping down the Avon to an urgent new rendezvous.

"But you aren't in it, though, are you?" she said to Hamish, frowning. "I don't remember seeing you. With your beautiful fair hair, you'd be awfully good, you know. Even if it was only a small part. Mind you, I can even see you as Hamlet the Prince, you know. I don't want to criticise, but to be truthful we did think maybe a younger actor would have been more suitable? Someone like you?"

She smiled winningly at him, her head on one side. Hamish saw she'd been a beauty perhaps thirty or more years ago, when she would have been slim and naturally blonde. Since then the combined skills of a hairdresser, a cosmetic surgeon and a dietician had not been entirely successful in holding back the tide of time, he thought.

Hamish smiled politely at her.

"I am what is called cover, madam," he said. "What used to be known as an understudy in less enlightened days. I learn all the lines and the moves and attend every rehearsal, but never actually appear. It's terrific fun."

"Oh, how exciting," said the woman. "And whose part do you cover?"

"Oh, whoever's part seems to be in need of it," said Hamish. Olivia dropped her head and stared at him under lowered eyelids. Oz, who had been stirring uneasily on his seat, suddenly leapt up. His hand delicately inspected the seat of his tight trousers.

"What – the – hell is that stain? I thought I could feel something damp."

"Oh, sorry, sorry, soz, soz, soz," said Olivia. "So soz, Oz! I warned Ham about these mulberries, but I forgot to tell you!"

"*You horrid thing!* Now I hate mulberry trees! I shall never get that mark out," Oz cried. "I shall never like a mulberry tree ever again! And these chinos are only second time on. Beastly tree."

Hamish was trying not to giggle.

"*So soz, Oz,*" he mimicked. "And they fit you so well, Oz! Maybe you can make a feature of it? *The Stain of the Mulberry* on your bottom. Start a fashion."

The middle-aged couple had returned to their table. The woman was saying to her husband, "Lovely boy, isn't he? Now that's how I imagine Hamlet..."

Olivia flashed them a radiant smile, but Oz glared balefully after them.

"I hate people like that," he said. "*How do you learn all those lines?* It's your job, for Christ's sake. You don't ask a dentist how he learnt to pull teeth or an undertaker how..."

Olivia interrupted hastily.

"And then we're going to Shakespeare's tomb. You can come with us if you like."

"Shakespeare's tomb? Been there, done that, thanks," said Oz, settling himself down as best he could on the uncomfortable bench. "Prepare to be disappointed. So, you're not among the *Who Wrote Shakespeare?* school then? *Find the mystery playwright? This guy couldn't possibly have been the poet*, etc.?"

"Oh God, not all that Bacon, de Vere, Elizabeth I business surely?" groaned Olivia. "I thought all that rubbish about Shakespeare not being aristocratic enough to write about real life was old hat these days."

"Oh, I don't know, sweetie," said Oz, picking up his orange juice. "There are quite a few mysteries to be answered about our Mr Shaxpur from Stratford, if that's your inclination. The man with no literary connections whatsoever, for a start. You should talk to Polly, shouldn't she, Ham? Anyway, never mind that. There's something I've been meaning to ask. How did you two meet? You obviously knew each other before."

"We were at RADA together," said Olivia. "Weren't we, honey bun? Ham was the rising star after reading English at Oxford…"

"…who fizzled out after RADA and went off on a gap year to Italy," finished Hamish. "I was just one of Ol's many admirers. She won all the awards and then got into telly. The rest is history. But when we both happened to get cast by the RSC, we met again and kind of hit it off. It must have been in our stars, don't you think?"

Olivia interrupted him, pointing at the time on her phone. She stood up and pulled on a top, exposing some of her suntanned back as she did so. She was conscious of several pairs of male eyes swivelling robotically towards her.

"Come on, fellow thespians," she said quickly. "Enough hot air and history. It's after two, and we're in rehearsal again at four. Act Two. Full dress. That woman cannot let it go. Griselda knows there's something basically wrong with the production, but she's too star-struck to face up to it. You'd better be lurking around too, Ham. You know what our delightful director is like if you've skived off."

"Certainly do," said Hamish. "Dear Griselda. Nothing better she likes than to kick poor old bloody cover when she's looking for a whipping boy. She daren't criticise her precious Sir of course – he might melt." They all laughed.

6

Hamish and Olivia strolled along the riverside path past the two big theatres, the Royal Shakespeare Theatre with its fine art deco features, and its Victorian Gothic neighbour, the Swan Theatre. It had been a week of hard work, and they were ready for a break. The sun was already hot on their faces and arms as they walked hand in hand. They mingled with the tourists, many of whom appeared to be Japanese or Chinese, nearly all engaged in taking photographs. *"Shall I compare thee to a summer's day?"* carolled Hamish, looking into Olivia's upturned face. She looked exceptionally pretty today, he thought. She had caught the sun, and her blonde hair was fashionably streaked, without the aid of a hair stylist. *"Thou art more lovely and more temperate. Sometimes too hot the eye of heaven shines…"*

Olivia smiled. She was relieved to see Hamish relaxed and happy. Whereas she was on stage almost every night, enjoying excellent reviews, poor Hamish often had little to do as an understudy except to hang around. He couldn't relax in case the Sir was ill, and had to be ready to stand in at short notice, word perfect and fully rehearsed. The strain was depressing him, but he was determined not to show it. Olivia took his arm and joined in.

"And summer's lease hath all too short a date."

"You're telling me. Summer will be over soon. Time's just flying by."

He gave her a look, and she let him recite the remainder of the sonnet, enjoying his fine voice and skilful delivery.

"...But thy eternal summer shall not fade,
When in immortal lines to Time thou grow'st.
So long as men can breathe, or eyes can see,
So long lives this, and this gives life to thee."

Hamish paused and looked at her.

"I know he's praising her (or is it him?), but do you realise the great thing about those last lines? He knew! Shakespeare *knew* that his genius would last forever. I find that really consoling, given that there is so little known about him."

"Oh, come on!" laughed Olivia. They had reached the churchyard on an overgrown path through shrubbery. "We know plenty about him. Just read all the books about his life."

They went into the church. It was more than a place of worship now, with its shop and notice boards, as befits one of the most visited churches in England. They read:

"Built in 1210 on the foundation of a Saxon monastery. Visit the grave of William Shakespeare, buried next to his wife Anne Hathaway, his eldest daughter Susannah, and other members of his family."

At the entrance to the chancel was a large blue sign reading, "This Way to Shakespeare's Grave". A lady welcomed them pleasantly to the tombs. They duly paid the entrance fee and joined an excited queue of visitors from several continents.

Finally, they were admitted to the chancel to gaze down at a line of five tombstones on the floor. The graves of Anne Shakespeare, William Shakespeare, Thomas Nash, John Hall and Susannah Hall were all clearly marked out, lying neatly side by side.

"Very tidy," said Hamish, turning away and peering about the chancel. "Is there anything about his plays anywhere? Quotations or something?"

"Don't forget that inscription on the tombstone on the floor. Presumably he wrote that." Olivia pointed down.

"Good friend for Jesus' sake forbear,

to dig the dust enclosed here.

Blessed be the man that spares these stones,

And cursed be he that moves my bones!"

Hamish chanted it aloud in a suitably sepulchral voice.

"My God, not his finest effort. In fact, if Shakespeare wrote that himself as his epitaph, I'll eat my doublet and hose. That's just doggerel someone's put on the tomb to stop souvenir hunters sticking their noses in. Doesn't even mention his name."

"Perhaps his wife wrote it after he died," said Olivia.

"Well, you might say that, but I couldn't possibly comment! Somebody who didn't want anyone poking around too much, that's for sure. I wonder why."

"I must admit the whole thing does feel a bit staged, with those tombstones all in a row," Olivia admitted. She shuddered. "And that horrid bust of him..."

"Didn't someone describe him as looking like a self-satisfied pork butcher?" said Hamish.

"Yes, I'm sure he had a much nicer face than that. Well, here's the monument underneath. Can you read what it says? I can't."

They squinted at it through the barrier, but it was too far away.

"Here's the transcription," said a helpful guide. They had seen him talking to a small group of schoolchildren and their teacher, who were standing with awestruck expressions in front of the monument. He gave the young couple a card, which they tried to read.

Hamish said, "I can't make much sense of it, to be honest. It says his name doth deck the tomb, but it doesn't, does it? And then it ends:

Far more than cost: since all that he hath writ,

Leaves living art, but page, to serve his wit.

I haven't a clue what that means."

They turned to the guide for elucidation. He was a youngish man, tall and slim, with a ready smile.

"Yes, it's intriguing, isn't it? Some people say it's a cypher or code. The Elizabethans were very keen on them. The most famous cryptographer was a man named John Dee, and there is a school of thought that says he wrote this. But we just don't know." He shrugged his shoulders and gestured with his hand towards the tomb.

"The year 1623 is an *annus mirabilis* in the story of Shakespeare, seven years after he died. It was when the First Folio was published. At that time, the tomb took on its present appearance, along with the admittedly rather odd inscription and the tombstones laid out. You can see the famous bust of William Shakespeare, showing him holding a quill pen. Oddly enough, an earlier contemporary drawing of it shows him holding a woolsack, the symbol of a merchant, and not a pen at all. That too was probably altered in 1623."

"That's when it all happened, after he died? Till then he was only known as a businessman? Ah well, it's fascinating stuff," said Hamish.

He was looking exaggeratedly interested, hanging on to the guide's every word. Olivia knew the signs. They meant he was getting bored and then there would be trouble. Hamish could get very irritating. Was she getting just a bit too fond of him? Surely not. Once this season was over they would no doubt go their separate ways, just bumping into each other occasionally. The world of acting was like that. Best to enjoy it while it lasted.

"It's a fine church too, and there's so much to look at. And it's such a wonderful feeling to be in the very church where he was buried," she said quickly, taking Hamish's arm. "Shall we go and see Hall's Croft now? John Hall, who married Susanna, was Shakespeare's son-in-law and physician. Just down this street. We'll find out a bit more about him there." She turned to the guide, melting him with her smile. "Thank you so much for your time. It's been *so* interesting."

She could be quite the *grande dame* sometimes, thought Hamish. But only in the nicest possible way. He smiled and squeezed her hand as they left the church and wandered out into the sunshine, a little way down the road to a handsome half-timbered Jacobean house. A glimpse through a gap in a gate revealed inviting-looking gardens.

They showed their Shakespeare Birthplace Trust pass at the entrance and went in. The lovely house had been immaculately restored, as they had come to expect of the Trust. Each room included a small exhibition of the medical and surgical practices of the time.

Hamish was studying a card.

"I see that Dr Hall was interested in using plants to cure diseases and had studied over 100 different herbs in his researches. His case notes and list of patients is exhibited – ah, here we are. The poet Michael Drayton was one of his patients. Sadly, Shakespeare's name is not among the list. Ah well."

7

Let me see. (*Takes the skull*)
Alas, poor Yorick!
I knew him, Horatio, a fellow of infinite jest, of most excellent
fancy. He hath borne me on his back a thousand times, and now
- how abhorred in my imagination it is! My gorge rises at it.
Act V, scene i

Twenty minutes later, after a tour of the medical exhibits, Hamish and Olivia emerged from the house to sit in the beautifully kept gardens and enjoy the sun. Bees and butterflies were busying themselves among the bushes, and two fat pigeons cooed lovingly at each other.

"We're doing a good job," said Hamish. "We've been to Shakespeare's birthplace, his school, his grave, and now his daughter's house. All lovely places, full of happy tourists. We're not learning an awful lot about his work though, are we? Is he a bit of a mystery man, do you think?"

"What do you mean? It's clear enough to me. Has Polly been filling your head with rubbish?"

Hamish smiled and turned away, scratching his head. The midges were dancing round in the sunshine and he was being bitten.

"Well, I suppose I'm just curious why nobody in his lifetime mentioned that the greatest playwright in the world happens to be living here in Stratford. It was a very small town then, hardly more than a village, after all. But it seems he was known only as a local land and property owner, and a money lender."

"Times were different then," said Olivia, irritated by the course of the conversation and taking out her phone again. "Perhaps they didn't bother with that sort of thing in his day. He came back here from London to relax and kept his identity quiet."

"Could be," agreed Hamish, enjoying the sun on his face. "He was just as much a mystery in London as well, of course. Almost as if he deliberately concealed any traces of himself. We know plenty about his literary contemporaries. Even when he died, no-one seems to have noticed at all. Most of the other poets of the time were buried in Westminster Abbey, in Poets' Corner. But all the poor old Bard got was that tomb seven years later, and that pork butcher's bust over there." He gestured towards the roof of the church beyond the neatly trimmed hedges.

"Oh, for heavens' sake," said Olivia. "The man died over four hundred years ago. What do you expect to find, parchments everywhere? Quill pens with ink on them drying in the sun? Yorick's skull dug up in his garden?"

"No, I'm just saying, okay, he clearly was a prominent citizen in Stratford. No question. Loads of documentation about that. Married a local girl and so on. And we know he'd been an actor in London. It's just the writer bit seems very thin on the ground to say the least, that's all." Hamish leapt up suddenly. "Never mind. I'm starving. Shall we go and eat somewhere? Dirty Duck? Or shall we go into town? No, what about that new…"

Olivia sighed and put her phone away. The gardens had filled with visitors chattering away in different languages. Some of them might be glad of a place on the wooden bench. Waiting for Hamish to come to a decision about something was not for the fainthearted.

"It doesn't seem to worry anybody else, does it?" she said, standing up. "Stratford is a magical place because of Shakespeare, as far as I'm concerned." She gathered up her things. "Yes, I fancy a snack, and you can treat me to a long cold glass of Carlsberg in the Duck, on condition you stop ranting, okay?"

"As a matter of fact, I can name you twenty famous people who worry about it too, if you want to know. Sigmund Freud. Mark Twain. Orson Welles. John Gielgud. Daphne du Maurier, your favourite author, Ted Hughes for another…" Hamish protested, until Olivia's hand wrapped firmly round his mouth.

"That's quite enough. Let's go."

They set off down the riverside walk to the pub, the summer sun hot on their heads, while the ducks quacked and quarrelled on the banks of the Avon like fishwives haggling in the marketplace. They diverted a little to pass the theatre, which stood boldly against the sky, a glorious monument to the Bard.

A steady stream of people was going in and out of the big entrance doors. Huge mounted posters outside it advertised the two current productions, which alternated. One showed Olivia's face five times larger than life-size, gazing soulfully up at the Sir. This had given her a real thrill at first, but she had begun to find it embarrassing.

"Oh, look! There's a big pigeon sitting over your head!" said Hamish. "I hope he's showing you due respect."

"In the only way he can, I suppose," said Olivia. "Shoo! That's my face you're pooing on." She flapped her arms, and the bird flapped its wings in response. It flew a few feet further off, looking aggrieved to be interrupted at its toilet. They laughed and retraced their steps back to the Dirty Duck. No-one in the pub apart from the bar staff gave any sign of recognising her, which was a relief. And the lager was welcome too with some nibbles.

"Just a half for me. I'm on tonight. Will you be in?" said Olivia. As long as they were within call, understudies didn't have to attend every performance once the play was running. Hamish had picked up a newspaper someone had left on a table and was scanning the sports pages.

"You haven't been in for ages," she continued. "The director, in her inimitable way, has touched on your absence once or twice. You two really don't hit it off, do you?"

"Who, darling little Griselda? *I will speak daggers to her, but use none.* I'll come in tonight, if only for the pleasure of watching you make love to the Sir."

"Yeah, right. At least we're off tomorrow though, thank goodness. There will be three days of *All's Well that Ends Well*. Don't forget we're going to Polly's for supper on Sunday, by the way."

"Mm. Should be interesting. He's going to tell us some more about what he calls the authorship mystery. If you get fed up with his lecturing, you'll just have to close your ears." Hamish put the paper back on the table.

"Oh, Polly's old school. He'll probably send me out to the kitchen to do the washing up, while the men talk about the important stuff."

"Jolly good show!" said Hamish in his best public school tones. "Let's hope he's got some vintage port and the best Havanas."

"Whatever," said Olivia. Hamish smiled. "As we're off tomorrow, do you fancy getting some fresh air? It looks like being another nice day. You know the Greenway? The old disused railway line, goes to Long Marston apparently. It's a bridleway and cycle path now. Oz told me you can hire bikes there for the day if you like."

"Sounds good to me," said Olivia. "Great idea. Tell you what – why don't we invite Oz to come with us? Unless he's off on another jaunt to Brum, of course. I'll ask him this evening. Anyway, we must get on. I want to get in early tonight."

They gingerly descended the steep steps that led from the Dirty Duck to the road and headed back to their flat.

8

**O thou my lovely boy, who in thy power
Dost hold Time's fickle glass, his sickle hour**
Sonnet 126

Their spirits were high as the three actors set off on their hired bikes down the old railway track. The river ran below them at a stately pace near the popular little racetrack. Almost immediately they came to an iron bridge, corroded and multi coloured. The sun was shining and the sky was blue and cloudless, which contributed to their high spirits. In the fields, the crops were starting to grow and here and there scarlet poppies punctuated the green like spots of blood.

Olivia's new white shorts were well cut and skimpy, showing off her tanned legs. Oz had produced a yellow and black Lycra cycling outfit, calculated to flatter his toned physique. Hamish was proud of his two companions, and his mood had lifted above the gloom induced by his frustration with his current career. They bunched together at first, but after a few hundred metres Hamish pulled ahead.

"Well, Oz," he said over his shoulder, as they sped along the cycle path, past well-kept fields and summer woods. "How are your Shakespearean studies going?"

"Oh, I've given myself a cool task," said Oz. "I've been

reading all the sonnets, from first to last. And very stimulating they are too."

"Stimulating in what way?" asked Hamish. "To be honest, I've never read them all. Just the three or four obvious ones. *My mistress' eyes are nothing like the sun. Coral is far more red than her lips' red…*"

"All right, all right," said Olivia quickly from behind. "We get the picture. Mind this crossing." The railway line cut across their path at this point, and they rode over the tracks. "Well, for a start, I'd never realised he was so gay. And passionate with it! Fair turned me on, loike." Oz had dropped into a Brummie accent, his latest acquisition since spending some of his days off in Birmingham. He had told Hamish he'd exhausted the gay scene in Stratford, and had no steady partner.

"He wrote some of them to the Dark Lady though, didn't he?" asked Olivia.

"Of course," said Oz, "but only a couple of dozen. Like the one Ham's just quoted. The rest were to his 'Lovely Boy'. Oh my dears, was he wild about him. He must have been quite something." He giggled and fiddled with the gear lever on his handlebars.

"What do we know about the boyfriend then?" asked Hamish. "Bugger all as usual I suppose, as we have come to expect from our mystery poet."

"Oh, well, we know the boyfriend's name at least," said Oz unexpectedly. "Or his first name anyway. Not much mystery about that. It was Will. 'Sonnet 135' mentions it thirteen times – in one sonnet!"

"And 'will' meant sexual desire too, didn't it?" said Hamish. "Ooh, aren't we precious? Yes, it certainly meant that too.

So he could use that as a pun."

"Interesting," said Hamish, skilfully negotiating round a large pothole. "Look out here! What else do they tell us?"

"Well, the poet seemed to be pretty unhappy about something, and generally out of favour with the Royal Court. They were the big movers and shakers in those troubled political times. There's a theory he was imprisoned in the Tower of London for a while. *When in disgrace with fortune and men's eyes, I all alone beweep my outcast state…* And he was lame. Mentions it more than once."

"But *mad about the boy*?" said Hamish in his best Noel Coward voice. The men slowed down to pass a family with two dogs who were taking up most of the path, then cycled side by side.

"Totally besotted. He tells him so again and again," said Oz. "He loved Will with a feverish intensity. But sadly it doesn't look as if his love was reciprocated. Merely tolerated, perhaps. And the young man didn't appreciate the sonnets. 'Sonnet 48' says so through gritted teeth… *but thou, to whom my jewels trifles are.* He refers to his poems as jewels more than once."

"Pearls before swine?" said Hamish, leaning forward over his handlebars like a competitor in the Tour de France, then pushing ahead again. "Hey, this is the life!"

"Oh, that is *so* sad," said Olivia, screwing up her face and pushing back her fair hair from her eyes. Now they were riding three abreast as the path of the old railway line widened. "Ham, ease back a bit, for God's sake. Those wonderful poems not appreciated? But what about the Dark Lady – perhaps she was more receptive."

"One would hope so," said Oz. "Either way he didn't seem

to have had much luck with the objects of his passion."

Swallows were flying overhead doing acrobatics in the sky, which was a deep azure blue. A few cotton wool clouds offered a contrast here and there on the canvas of the supreme artist.

"So he played for both teams, did he?" said Hamish, feeling his muscles complaining. He really ought to go to the theatre gym more often. "Kicked both ways?"

"How very dare you!" Oz giggled. "Oh yes indeed. Our Bard was a real Betty-both-ways. It's very common, you know. You'd be surprised how many of my gay friends are married. One of them chooses what he wants his wife to wear the next day and lays the clothes out on their bed."

Hamish, whose parents were divorced, said nothing. Marriage was sometimes a sore topic with him.

"*Ha ha.* That's appalling, Oz! Wouldn't do for me," giggled Olivia. "Hamish wouldn't notice if I wore a bin liner. So the Bard loved the Dark Lady as well as the boy?"

"It would seem so. But the one I'd like to know more about is Will, his *beauteous and lovely youth,*" said Oz. "He must have been quite something to inspire such love."

"Yes, I wonder how they met?" said Hamish. "Presumably in the world of the theatre. Perhaps he was a fellow member of the company, an actor? What was he like, the boy, do you think - any idea?"

"Oh, exceptional, obviously, to have inspired the Bard's devotion. Very attractive, clever, quick to learn. Perhaps did a bit of writing himself. Maybe Polly will have something to say about it when we go to his place for supper."

"Interesting. Hey, that looks like Long Marston down there.

Well-known WW2 airfield, wasn't it? Shall we have a look?"

The heat of the day hung heavily on them, drenching them in sweat, as they turned their wheels down towards the village to give their aching muscles a break. A little cafe beckoned around the corner, its sign promising cream teas, a sure way to the heart of any English visitor.

"Never mind the sonnets," Olivia said. "I just want tea. Wonder if they do cake as well?"

9

Excellent, i' faith, of the chameleon's dish.
I eat of the air, promise-crammed! You cannot feed capons so
Act 3, scene ii

"What's this meant to be?" said Polly, wrinkling his nose fastidiously as he opened the door to Olivia and Hamish. He held the bottle they offered him at arm's length. "Chateau Superstore? You really shouldn't fall for these cheap plonks – hoicked up to twice the real price and then stuck in the Bargain Bin, you know. Oldest trick in the supermarket's books."

Hamish was put out but tried not to show it. He'd actually spent nearly £15 on the wine instead of his usual five and was sorry now that he'd bothered.

"Well, let's open it and see what it tastes like, shall we?" said Olivia tactfully, as they crowded into the little room that opened straight off the street. She picked up a corkscrew off the table and set to work.

Across the road through the bullseye glass window they could see the playgoers already crowding the steps to the theatre entrance. The buzz of expectation was audible from the cottage. There was nowhere quite like the RSC anywhere else in the world of drama, she thought. To watch Shakespeare in his very own hometown, and what's more, to be a part of it, actually to be Ophelia in *Hamlet*…

Sometimes she thought it must all be a dream. She just hoped there wouldn't be a rude awakening.

"Come along, sit yourselves down," said Polly impatiently, his face red from his exertions in the kitchen. He wore a luridly patterned floral shirt, a little too tight for him, and an apron with the slogan 'Yes, Chef!'. A cigarette burned in an ashtray on the draining board. Wine and cooking were Polly's biggest hobbies after classical literature, and he took them both very seriously.

"Oz is already well stuck into my finest Montrachet."

Oz was in fact sitting quietly at the end of the sofa, sipping white wine from a beautiful crystal glass with a long stem, and leafing through a book he'd picked from the overflowing bookshelves. He looked more handsome than ever, a study in black and white with just a splash of imperial purple, shiny oxblood brogue shoes completing the ensemble. He smiled sweetly up at them.

"*What do you read, my lord?*" enquired Olivia.

"*Words, words, words*… Shakespeare's *Sonnets* again, actually. Can't get enough of them."

Polly brought out dishes of tempting hors d'oeuvres and left his guests to distribute them while he returned to the kitchen. As they helped themselves to seafood nibbles of prawns and scallops, cheese straws, tapenade with home baked bread, and large stuffed green Mediterranean olives, the little room filled with theatrical chatter and waspish gossip.

"I got some oysters today in the new deli," called Polly. "It's got a good fish counter. But then I decided they might

45

offend your delicate palates. They looked so delicious, I ate them myself at lunchtime. Made myself oyster *vermicelli*. Yummy!"

"That's all right by me," said Olivia, wrinkling her nose. "I can't stand the things. Never eat anything that's still alive, is my motto."

"And a very good one too. Certainly works for me with pigs," said Hamish.

"They can give you a nasty kick if you try and take a bite out of their legs."

Olivia giggled.

"Polly, this tapenade is del-ic-i-ous."

"Recipe I found last summer in Antibes, in the market," called Polly from the kitchen. "With a special added ingredient, of course. No, I am sworn to secrecy."

"This Montrachet's pretty good too," proclaimed Hamish, smacking his lips and holding his already empty glass up to the light. The theatrical gossip continued.

"The Sir's too old for the part. Hamlet's meant to be twenty-three, not fifty-three. No wonder the Sir's slathered in make-up."

"He's got a great voice, and he does project it well," said Oz. "But, okay, he's way over the top. The guy who put the ham in Hamlet. Ha ha. Anyway, you're only jealous."

"Of course I'm bloody jealous," said Hamish, picking up a fresh bottle. "Shall I dish this around, Polly? Ol? Some more? Yes, I know every line of that part, every inflection. All I need is a chance to prove myself."

"Patience, patience, dear boy. Your time will come," said Polly, coming in with dishes of delicious smelling Vichyssoise and setting them on the table. "Here we are. Made with asparagus instead of chicken. Sit down and enjoy, my children."

The soup was followed by the promised duckling, greeted with oohs and ahs by the company. They tucked in heartily, banter flying and wine flowing. Mozart's Serenade in D major was playing quietly in the background, as announced by Polly in a muttered aside.

This is the life, thought Hamish. Fine food, wine, and good company, by the Avon. He raised his glass.

"Here's to the chef!" he said. "And to the memory of the blessed Bard, without whom none of us would have a job."

They all clinked glasses to join in the toast.

"To the chef! And to the Bard!"

"My pleasure!" said Polly, a beam of satisfaction cracking his lined bearded face in spite of his best efforts to remain severe. "Good to see you all, dilettante wastrels though you are. Let's enjoy the meal, and we can talk a little about Mr W. S. afterwards if you would like to. But tell me the latest on the Sir? I hear he and madam had a big set-to? I must have missed it. What was all that about, Ham?"

"Well, he wanted to give his '*O what a rogue and peasant slave*' direct to the audience, gazing soulfully into the middle distance across the auditorium, but she said…"

Polly was passing round second helpings of the duckling as the discussion continued and had opened yet another bottle of wine. Olivia noted that the one she had opened had been left ignored in the kitchen and shrugged.

"Did you hear that the Sir demanded his dressing room be redecorated yet again?" she said. "Apparently, he still wasn't satisfied with the colour scheme. Considering that I'm

47

crammed into a tiny space no bigger than a boot cupboard, with Ros and Gill… Roll on the re-building plan, I say. Proper backstage facilities please!"

"You young ones won't believe this, but I can remember when Rosencrantz and Guildenstern were played by men," said Polly. "Yes, honestly! That was in the glory days when we did The Bard as he wrote it, instead of what some arty farty director dreams up."

"Got to move with the times, Polly," said Hamish, helping himself to the last of the duckling. "That's nothing to what it will be like after they've spent £100 million on the place. The Transformation Project, it's called, isn't it? It will issue in a new era, you mark my words. You'll have women playing all the main parts, Macbeth will be Nigerian – sorry, Oz! – and the Forest of Arden will have moved to Ho Chi Minh City."

"Sounds good to me," said Oz. "I'm all for the Revolution. We've had more than enough of pale stale males running everything. Give us girls a chance, I say!"

They all laughed and the conversation swept on, the volume increasing along with the wine intake until the cottage was abuzz with chatter.

10

It is as easy as lying. Look you, these are the stops.
But these cannot I command to any utterance of harmony.
I have not the skill.
Act III, scene 2

"So, it's like this," said Polly. They had cleared away the meal but were now sitting back in the little front room. Filtered coffee had appeared, along with a bottle of fine Armagnac, and Oz was rolling joints for anyone who wanted one. The other two were looking over at Polly.

"I hate to spoil anyone's illusions, but in this scenario, there are in fact two different men. So, firstly we have our local hero, Willie Shaxpur from Stratters."

He took a sip from his glass.

"This is what we actually know. Local man, got married at 18 to Anne Hathaway who was pregnant, had three children very quickly, no sign of much education if any. He went up to London in about 1587 when he was twenty-three, and worked as an actor. But incredibly, he came back to Stratford less than ten years later with an unexplained shedload of money and bought New Place, possibly the biggest house in town."

Hamish frowned.

"That *is* good going."

"Yes, and nobody's ever come up with a reasonable explanation of how he made so much money so quickly. Certainly not by writing plays at £5 a time if he was lucky, not a fortune even then. Anyway he kept himself busy thereafter doing various property transactions and being a respectable citizen. He did keep interests in London though, and later bought a share in the Globe Theatre. Died in Stratford in 1616 and may have been buried in the churchyard." He cleared his throat. "Apart from a few mundane property and tax transactions, there's honestly not a lot more known. Yes, there are over seventy documentary records of him as a businessman, but as you know, not one refers to him as an author in any way."

"It's quite extraordinary."

"Yes, Ham. And when he died he left no books, writings, letters, not even a scrap of paper. It seems that to the townsfolk of Stratford, he was a man with no connection with literature whatsoever. And at that time the population of Stratford was only about 1500 people, barely bigger than a village. Not a word was said about him being a writer until several years after his death. It is one of the biggest literary mysteries of all time. But very few people realise it."

Polly lit another cigarette and looked round the table to see if his audience was with him so far. Satisfied, he continued.

"There are a few bits of gossip from the period. One commentator says that as a boy Will was caught poaching deer at Charlecote Manor, another that he died under Bidford bridge after too good a night out in the pub with

Michael Drayton and the sainted Ben Jonson, whatever they were doing up here in the sticks."

"Will left his poor wife his second-best bed, didn't he?" asked Olivia. "And their son Hamnet died aged eleven."

"Absolutely. But we know nothing else about the marriage, except that none of his family could sign their own names. His father, and his daughter Susanna signed their names with an X."

"There really is so little known. That's why the Shakespeare story can seem a bit light on solid facts sometimes, I suppose," said Hamish. "I must admit I have noticed that it's very often 'might have', 'would have', 'may have', 'is thought to have' everywhere we go in the town, rather than anything definite."

Polly spread his hands.

"That's right. That is very noticeable. But nevertheless the tourist locations can be reasonably associated with William Shaxpur, the man who was only declared to the world as Shakespeare, the playwright, seven years after his death. He lived here all right, as did Anne Hathaway, and a very good reconstruction has been made of their life and times. The Birthplace Trust, for instance, does a wonderful job. But if the guidebooks stop short of stating too many certainties, that's as it should be."

"Anyway, it doesn't mean our man didn't write the plays," objected Hamish. "He must have written at least some of them here and popped up and down to London to see them put on."

Oz squealed.

"*Eek!* You didn't just *pop down* to London at that time,

you know! It meant a journey on horseback of at least five, maybe six days on bumpy unmade roads. Down to Moreton-in-Marsh, across to Oxford, and then another two or three days travelling. No M40, you know, or fast trains. No stagecoaches yet even, just horses. Oooh – *very* hard on the buttocks, I should imagine."

He shuddered and made an exaggerated moue of discontent. Polly laughed and poured out more drinks for his guests.

"Doesn't make much sense, I agree. But I haven't touched on the main problem yet. The astonishing breadth of the writer's learning and knowledge means that he had had an immensely good education from an early age. Almost certainly he must have gone to Oxford or Cambridge or both and studied law and philosophy among other subjects. He must have travelled extensively abroad and he knew several languages. Many of the plays are set in Italy, and his acquaintance with that country suggests the writer had lived there for a time. And please don't tell me he might have met Italian sailors in a dockside pub who could have furnished him with all this information. That is a joke. He was clearly infatuated with Italy, and that couldn't happen if he'd never been there."

Polly paused, then went on. He was a fluent lecturer, and revelled in having an audience. It reminded Olivia of her own days as a student, and she shifted uncomfortably in her seat at the memory of hours of boredom.

"In addition to that, the Bard's familiarity with the procedures of the Elizabethan Royal Court strongly suggests that he was an integral part of it. Virtually all his heroes are kings, queens or emperors, never commoners. It is the setting he was at ease with. In short, he was a man of rank. Sorry, but there it is."

The listeners all stirred, and there was silence for a moment. Oz was the first to speak.

"So what about poor young Will from Stratford. Couldn't he have had such an education?"

Polly shook his head.

"No, not a chance. Not a hope in hell. There is not a scintilla of evidence for it."

A sudden sharp bang startled the diners.

"*Rubbish*! This is all pure supposition, Polly!"

Everyone looked at Olivia, who had rapped her glass on the table nearly hard enough to crack it.

"Oh, I hate all this," she said crossly. "It makes me so angry. It's just intellectual snobbery. He was obviously an ordinary man with an extraordinary genius, for God's sake. Get over it!"

"Yes, he went to a good grammar school, didn't he, Polly?" said Hamish. And who knows where he travelled to and what and where he studied afterwards? What about the famous missing years?"

"The breadth of the Bard's education was so enormous that it is impossible a local grammar school could have provided it," said Polly. "Just impossible. There were probably only two or three teachers here in Stratford, don't forget, and you left school aged fourteen in those days. As a matter of fact, the school rolls for that period are missing anyway, so we don't even know that he actually went there. Look, do you want a list of what the writer had an intimate knowledge of?"

He leant forward, ticking his points off on his long fingers. "The law and legal terms, the customs of the Royal Court, the sports of the nobility such as falconry, statecraft, classical philosophy and literature, at least three foreign languages, Italy's geography and customs, gardening, music, the arts, astronomy, medicine, navigation and seamanship, folklore, heraldry. Oh, and he had a vocabulary of over 30,000 words, as well as coining more than a thousand totally new ones!"

"Blimey," said Oz in mock Cockney. "Certainly mikes yer fink, don' it, Guv?"

For a moment there was silence as the three actors stirred their positions and pondered Polly's proposition.

11

Why may not that be the skull of a lawyer?
Where be his quiddities now, his quillities, his cases,
his tenures, and his tricks?
Act V, scene i

Hamish scratched his jaw.

"He certainly knew a lot about the law, I'll give you that. I was thinking that the other day. You know that bit in the Gravediggers' scene? Talk about expert knowledge."

"Oh, come on," said Olivia impatiently. "He's only got to chat to a couple of lawyers and scribble down terms they use. Writers do that all the time."

Polly frowned, started to say something, and then continued with his lecture.

"There's another thing too. There is no *web* connecting Shaxpur's life with incidents in the plays or poetry. We can't make any links between the man himself as revealed through his works with the scanty information that we have about his life events. That is unique in the literary world. Writers can't avoid giving themselves away in their writings. It's just not possible."

"But you've just said we know very little about him," objected Olivia. "For all we know, his life might have been full of the sort of dramas and experiences that the plays are about."

"What, while living in Stratford and doing up properties?" said Polly sarcastically. "Doesn't leave much time for studying law, living in Italy, and reading history and philosophy, let alone writing and perhaps even producing thirty-seven plays, does it?"

"Not forgetting writing the *Sonnets*," called Oz. He still had hold of his copy of the poems. "To my mind they are an insight into his soul, darlings. Maybe that's where you should be looking to find your answers, Polly. Wonderful meal, by the way."

Hamish and Olivia agreed. Oz sat back in his chair with a tolerant smile on his face, smoking his joint and enjoying the conversation. Polly sipped some water while his cooking was praised again. He raised his hands in thanks and let them flop down again by his side.

"Thanks, guys. It's all in the preparation. And the timing. Maybe that's why actors are often good cooks. Help yourselves to drinks or more coffee. No, no more for me, thanks. Hope this isn't all too boring for you all? I've said my piece now. Got that off my chest."

"It's not boring exactly," said Olivia, "just irritating. I'm afraid I don't really go along with it. Not my sort of thing. I just say the lines and try not to bump into the scenery."

They all laughed politely. Olivia was known to be a very dedicated and intelligent actress.

"But Ham knows loads about it. He has plenty of time to read too. Don't you, you poor darling?"

Hamish made a face at her.

"Certainly do. Tell me about it."

"Lucky to have an opportunity like this to learn your trade,"

Polly said sharply. "I happen to think you're a damn good actor actually. A star in the making, maybe. Who knows? But for now you'll have to bite your tongue. We all have to learn."

"He certainly looks the part, doesn't he, bless him," said Oz. "Absolutely gorgeous." He put his hand on Hamish's knee for a moment. "I like the way you say the lines and project your voice too. Don't see too much of that these days. Proper training pays off."

Hamish was flattered and embarrassed at the same time. "Charmed, I'm sure. Pray proceed, Polly. This is fascinating. I'm sure there's more."

He gently removed Oz's hand. Olivia smiled and reached for a mint. Oz let out a cloud of smoke. He passed his joint on to Olivia, who shook her head, and then to Hamish. Polly paused and looked around, not sure if the others were convinced. Hamish was thoughtfully trying to spear a piece of Roquefort onto a cocktail stick and failing.

12

There's hope a great man's memory may outlive his life half a year.
But, by 'r Lady, he must build churches then,
or else shall he suffer not thinking on, with the hobby-horse,
whose epitaph is "For, oh, for, oh, the hobby-horse is forgot."
Act III, scene ii

Only Olivia appeared to be listening.

"This is doing my head in, Polly," she said crossly. "I adore my Shakespeare, and I won't put up with this. As far as I'm concerned, he's still here in this town. I can see his shadow sometimes. And he really, really doesn't like us poking around at his memory. No, I'm serious. Bad things might happen."

Polly shrugged, and sipped more water. He looked all in, Olivia thought. Cooking the meal must have taken it out of him. But she still felt cross.

Hamish smiled.

"Look, Ol, relax. Whether he's right or wrong, it doesn't make any difference to the man's genius. No need to get your knickers in a twist. Don't you agree, Oz?"

Oz looked up.

"How very dare you? I make it a rule never to get my knickers in a twist," he said, affecting a camp toss of the head before immersing himself again in the *Sonnets*. The

58

others laughed.

"I was just trying to give you a general background," Polly continued. "If it upsets you, I'll stop. I don't actually want to be a spoilsport. Just on my hobby horse, that's all."

"For O, for O, the hobby horse is forgot," quoted Olivia. "Yes, let's move on, shall we? While I've still got some illusions left."

"For Ol, for Oz, the hobby horse is forgot perhaps, but not for me," said Hamish. "We don't have to believe it. As we all agree, at the end of the day the plays and the poems are the only things that matter."

Olivia was sipping her coffee.

"Anyway, maybe it's true we don't know much about him, but I'm sure that's equally true of many other writers and artists at that time, isn't it, Polly?"

"No, I'm afraid it's not. We know quite a lot about all the other writers of any note from that period. Where they went to school, where they lived, along with original manuscripts, letters, books owned, and personal references from other people. But about William Shakespeare – literally nothing. It is beyond weird."

Olivia shrugged.

"Well, that was obviously his choice. So why can't we leave it at that? Incidentally, how many others think our local man didn't write the plays? I assume this isn't just your private theory. Ham says there are others."

"Oh, just a few. Only Walt Whitman, Orson Welles, John Galsworthy, Sigmund Freud..." said Polly sarcastically. "Charlie Chaplin even. Ted Hughes. And what about the great Mark Twain? Twain said that *'So far as anybody actually knows or can prove, Shakespeare of Stratford-upon-Avon never wrote a play in his life.'* He even wrote a novel about the subject. And how about Henry James? *'I am haunted by the conviction that the divine William is the biggest and most successful fraud ever practised on a patient world.'* That's clear enough, isn't it? Yes, people have been questioning for years how this man can possibly have written the plays. And that includes several of our leading Shakespearean actors today."

"Yeah, I heard about that. Brave souls." Hamish looked around the room. The joint had turned to ash, and Oz was busy rolling another. Olivia was flicking through a magazine on the sofa. Hamish waved the bottle of wine around, but it seemed he was the only taker. Then he had a thought. "Okay, so what about all the Warwickshire dialect words and phrases in his works? They're a pretty good clue, aren't they, for God's sake?"

Olivia nodded eagerly in agreement. "Yes, I've heard that, Polly."

"Would that they existed, *mes braves,*" said Polly. "In fact there's not a single phrase in all the plays that has been shown to be in the local dialect. I'm afraid it's just another cosy myth. Like the other one about there being dozens of references to glove making in the plays, Shaxpur's father's trade. There's actually nothing about gloves, apart from some badinage in *The Merry Wives of Windsor.* Nor is the town of Stratford ever mentioned in the plays. Not once."

Oz screwed up his face.

"Hmm. That really is odd. Incidentally, you say our man left no literary traces, but you haven't mentioned his signatures. There are quite a few examples of those, aren't there?"

Polly snorted, and his lined face grew tetchier than ever.

"There are indeed six of them, all in the last four years of Shaxpur's life. On a lawsuit, on mortgage documents, and in his infamous will. Do you know, he spelt his own name differently in every case. Can you really believe that of the world's greatest writer?"

He stared at Hamish as though holding him responsible for this.

"They may even not all be by the same hand. They are all so badly formed that according to some experts, the signatory was semi-illiterate. There's not much comfort to be found in the signatures, I can assure you." Polly stood and reached up to the bookshelf. "Hang on, I can show you one."

After a moment he opened a page in a book, and handed it to Hamish with a look of distaste.

"Here you are," he said. "How would you like to read a whole playscript by a man who writes like that? Ben Jonson says he never blotted a line. Well, this chap certainly did!"

"Hm, I see what you mean," said Hamish, handing it to the others after a moment. "The William's all right, but that surname... Can you imagine deciphering manuscripts written in that hand? Pity the poor printer."

Polly nodded.

"Leaving all that aside though, it still begs the question: if the Bard wasn't our humble Stratford citizen, however he signed his name, then who did write the plays and the sonnets? Any ideas on that, anyone? More wine? Ol?"

Both Oz and Olivia shook their heads, Olivia impatiently. Hamish held his glass out, and they all sat back to hear more.

13

"Well, there's a separate big mystery," said Polly, fiddling with his almost empty glass. "The writer himself was just as mysterious as the man from Stratford, assuming they were two different people. As I've said, the London man seems to have been absolutely determined that nobody should know anything about him, not even his name."

He stared up at the low ceiling of the little room.

"Okay. Here's the bottom line. We know almost nothing about the real playwright. But there are of course hundreds of clues to his identity in his writings. The thirty-seven plays, the 154 sonnets, and the two long poems tell us all about him, the person. It must be so. But if you are looking for the faintest whiff of the man himself as he appeared to his contemporaries, you will find nothing."

"Ah, I think I'm beginning to get the picture," said Hamish slowly. "The Stratford element is part of a cover-up job then? This could be my homework."

Olivia winced aloud, half closing her eyes.

"Oh Ham, not a conspiracy theory, please! I can't bear it. Polly, do you mind if I'm very greedy, and finish off this delicious roulade? Can I lick the bowl?"

She didn't wait for permission. The men watched her silently for a moment, lost in their own thoughts. She looked so lovely in the dim light, a beautiful child at a tea party. Not the grand actress at all.

Then Hamish said, "So Polly, who in your opinion did write them then? Give me a lead. I'm going to go into this."

Polly seemed reluctant to answer this immediately.

"Well, Olivia is absolutely right," he said slowly. "It certainly was a conspiracy of silence of some sort. The Elizabethans were noted for them. A conspiracy to conceal the name of one man. As you know, there is no shortage of contenders. But to me one name stands out, one man who fits the bill in pretty well every particular. He has everything going for him that the Stratfordians would die for. An unparalleled education, intimate knowledge of the royal courts, an obsession with Italy, access to libraries, the wealth and leisure to devote to writing, a international reputation as a..., as a..." But it seemed that he had lost his track. He grimaced in pain, undid a button on his trousers and breathed out heavily. He closed his eyes, then he took a deep breath and resumed. His face had gone waxy, and a line of sweat had appeared on his forehead.

"Oof. That's better. Oh, the hell with it. Look it up if you're interested. His name was Edward de Vere. Earl of Oxford. And that's a fact."

Hamish felt that shiver down his spine again, and gulped. There was a long silence in the room. Polly was the first to break it.

"Help yourselves to more drinks and coffee. Put those revolting spliffs away and have a decent Havana cigar, Oz. And I've got some passable Cockburn's vintage port if anyone has a palate fine enough to try it?" He was speaking with an effort. "Would you excuse me please? Got to pay a visit. Talking too much."

They watched him go stiffly up the narrow staircase, his hand to his back, concern on their faces. Then Olivia stood up. "Told you so," she said, winking at Ham. "I know my place. Ladies' retirement time. I'll just make a start on these dishes in the kitchen while you gentlemen relax. If there was a drawing room, I'd discreetly withdraw to it and talk to myself about knitting patterns."

Hamish smiled and poured fresh glasses of Merlot for himself and Oz.

"What do you reckon, Oz?" he asked. "Polly seems to know his stuff. On the other hand, it seems pretty outrageous to suggest that this whole Stratford concept is a fiction, based on some false premise? All these millions of tourists… And who was this guy de Vere?"

He gestured through the window at the riverside walk, the huge bulk of the theatre now dimmer in the darkness. The weather had changed, and rain was sweeping across the concourse. The playgoers and the tourists had gone home and the theatre had closed its doors. He shook his head and smiled ruefully.

"Three million visitors a year can't be wrong, you mean?" Oz said, shrugging. "I don't think Polly is saying that. I've been reading about this. I know nothing about de Vere,

I'm afraid. That can be your homework, Ham. But the point is that the playwright's identity has been shrouded in mystery from day one, which nobody can deny. And that must have been deliberate on his part. The first fifteen plays were actually published anonymously. It's only after 1598 that they began to be ascribed to somebody. Namely *Mr William Shake-speare*, whose name began to appear as the author at that time. The hyphen almost always indicated a pseudonym, by the way. That's all we really know. No notes, no manuscripts, no drafts. Nothing in fact about his working practices at all."

"And he doesn't *want* us to know either!" called Olivia from the kitchen where she had been stacking up the dishes. She emerged wiping her hands elegantly on a Stratford-upon-Avon souvenir tea towel decorated with all the places associated with the Bard. It must have come with the furnished house, Olivia thought. She couldn't imagine Polly buying it.

"He obviously went to great lengths to keep himself unknown, and everybody else went along with it. Maybe he didn't want the paparazzi of the day after him!"

The two men laughed, and the conversation turned to theatre gossip. The rumours of a hugely ambitious development programme for the theatre, which would mean it being closed for a long period, were a matter of great concern to the actors. It was a time of uncertainty for them and the subject of much deep discussion. They paused and looked up when Polly finally came downstairs. He was white in the face.

"Sorry about that," he grunted. "Bit of a dodgy tummy. Conversation moved on, I hope? I was beginning to bore myself. Bit obsessed, I'm afraid."

"As a matter of fact, we were talking about something else," said Oz. "Could the theatre really close down for several years for re-building? And more importantly, is Griselda having it off with that pretty little wardrobe girl? I saw them having lunch together in Luxton's, and they looked very lovey-dovey."

"Isn't that a tradition in *Hamlet* productions?" said Olivia. "You mean like, 'Is Hamlet sleeping with Ophelia? Yes, but only on tour.' Ha ha. Old joke."

"Yes, well that isn't going to happen in this production!" laughed Olivia. "I think I'm safe enough with the Sir, don't you?"

Their laughter was interrupted by a groan from Polly, who was holding his stomach and whose face had gone from white to green.

"Going to be sick..." he managed to say and got to the kitchen sink just in time. The others looked at each other aghast.

"Good job you did wash up and clear the decks," said Hamish. "He must have had a lot more to drink than we realized."

Oz was in the kitchen with his arm round Polly's shoulders. He was still hunched over the sink.

"Better, old chap?" Oz said. "Too much of the old el vino? You want to come and sit down?" But Polly was being sick again, and Oz recoiled. "I don't think he had that much wine," he said over his shoulder. "More likely something he ate."

Olivia and Hamish looked at each other, the same thought forming in their minds.

"Didn't he say he'd eaten oysters at lunchtime?" said Olivia. "Polly? Is it the oysters, d'you think?"

Polly turned to them, his eyes tight closed.

"One or two of them tasted a bit funny," he managed to say. "I thought I'd spat them out. I... *oooff.*"

He turned back to the sink and retched again. Finally they helped him back to the sofa, trying to ignore the fact that he'd been sick down the front of his shirt.

"Are you in pain?" asked Olivia. "Just lie down."

'Yes. Here in my tummy." Polly arched his back. "And... here." He gripped his bottom with both hands. "*Argh.* Stabbing pain. Need to go to..."

He pulled himself off the couch and quickly went upstairs again. They could hear him groaning from the bathroom, and looked at each other, unsure what to do.

Then Oz took charge.

"Right, I'm getting an ambulance," he said, pulling out his phone. "This isn't funny. He's obviously got food poisoning. A bad oyster can be fatal. Hello. Hello? Yes, please. Ambulance." He gave the address.

"I told you Shakespeare's ghost wouldn't like it," Olivia said. "No, I'm being serious. Some secrets are better not probed." She shivered and pulled her arms around herself.

Oz had gone upstairs to help Polly, who judging by the sounds he was making was worse. They waited for the ambulance in an uneasy silence for some minutes, the jovial mood of the evening having completely evaporated. Then Hamish looked at Olivia with a wicked grin on his face.

"It's poetic justice, isn't it?" he said. "What happens to Polly – he gets stabbed in the arras, doesn't he? Well, this time it's in the arse! Geddit? Poetic justice for you. *The Revenge of the Bard!*"

"Ha ha. Very funny," said Olivia sarcastically. Sometimes she found Hamish immature and childish. She bit her lip, then looked up. A blue light was revolving in the street outside, and she quickly rose to open the door. The sky had turned pitch black, blacker than the night itself.

The theatre stood starkly against the skyline, dark clouds building steadily up ominously behind it. A hint of menace hung in the air.

Rain was soaking the uniformed figures standing on the doorstep. One man was tall and thin, the younger one shorter and bespectacled, silent harbingers of doom sent from the Gods. Above their heads thunder rumbled, and a sudden shaft of lightning lit up their unsmiling faces. The rain was torrential, bouncing off the empty pavements.

"You'd better come in," said Olivia. "He's not looking good at all."

14

**A certain robustious periwig-pated fellow is tearing
a passion to tatters**
Act III, scene ii

The Sir was in full cry.

"*You cannot, sir, take from me anything that I will more
willingly part withal— except my life, except my life, except
my life,*" he declaimed, going through the full gamut of
emotions as he did so.

But Griselda was not happy. She was tapping her notebook
on her thigh, and gnawing her lip, a habit she had when
under stress.

"Maybe pull that line back a little?" she ventured. "Throw
it away a bit?"

"Throw it away?" said the Sir, his eyes widening with
contempt. "This is Shakespeare, my dear woman. Not some
mumbled rubbish on the telly. Throw it away, indeed."

Griselda flapped a hand weakly and sat back on her
cushion. The fact that the celebrated actor was notorious
for his excessive gestures and exaggerated reactions was
apparent to everyone except the Sir himself. A large ego
and unassailable self-belief is impossible to counter.

Hamish was sitting with Horatio in aisle seats in the
rehearsal theatre, idly watching the director taking the Sir

and Polly's stand-in through their paces for the third time that morning. His nails were digging into his palms as he muttered to his companion.

"God, Horesh, I'm almost sorry for the bloody woman. She looks as if she'd like to murder him, but hasn't got the guts. Shakespeare couldn't be more explicit about ham acting, in the speech to the Players. And what does this mountebank do? Waves his arms around like a tic-tac man at Cheltenham on Gold Cup Day. Over-emphasising every word, as if we were all deaf or stupid."

Horatio had heard all this before. He was slim and dark, of Indian heritage, with a kind face and ready smile. He had known Hamish since they were at drama school together and was his greatest admirer. He sympathised so much with his friend's frustration at having to watch someone manhandle a part he would be so much better at himself. It was one of the everyday irritations of an actor's life.

"Steady on, Ham," he whispered. "You're talking about one of the world's greatest actors. It must be true, it says so in the programme."

"Oh, give me strength. Let's go and have a coffee, for God's sake."

"You go. I've got to hang on here. We're doing the scene with the Ghost again after this."

"Okay, pal. Have fun. Catch you later." Hamish put his hand on Horatio's shoulder and slipped out of the theatre to the cafe. He found Olivia tucking into a cake at one of the tables on the terrace. The restaurant was crowded with actors from *All's Well That Ends Well*, which was running as a matinee that afternoon. Hamish nodded to one or two friends as he made his way over to Olivia.

"How's it going in there?" she enquired.

"Don't ask. I'll just grab a coffee and join you. Ah, there's Oz."

"Hi there. How's Polly?" asked Oz, pushing his way towards them, a large mug of green tea in his hand. "Have you been to see him in hospital?"

"No, we haven't been able to get away," said Hamish. "We called them earlier this morning, and they said he was comfortable, as they always do. But it looks as if they're going to be keeping him in, comfortable or not. We must go and see him as soon as we possibly can."

"Food poisoning can be very nasty," said Oz. "What a bugger. After him cooking that wonderful meal for us. Can I join you?"

He moved Hamish's jacket off a chair which he had pulled up to the table.

"So what did you think of Dallas apart from that, Mrs Kennedy?" he said. Olivia raised her eyebrows questioningly.

Oz smiled.

"Old assassination joke. By which I mean, leaving aside Polly's indisposition for the moment, what did you make of his thesis?"

Hamish spread his hands.

"Well, if you're looking for someone of an aristocratic background, well-travelled, hugely learned, exceptionally well educated, as it seems we must, then to say that Master Will from Stratford is not your man is to put it mildly. So we have to look for someone else as TB."

"TB being the Bard, I suppose," said Oz. "So who was it? That's your project… and no doubt you'll let us know when you find out *whodunnit*. Are you going to finish that ginger cake, Ol?"

"No, help yourself," said Olivia, pushing her plate across the table. "I shouldn't eat it anyway. My one indulgence. So what's your take on it, Oz?"

Oz was silent for a moment while he ate. The others waited politely. Then he elegantly licked his fingers and wiped them on a tissue.

"To be honest," he said, "I'm more interested in the Stratford man, even if he didn't write the plays, if you see what I mean. All we really know about him is that he was an actor in London. And I think that must be very significant, though I can't yet quite see how at the moment. But what would be his connection with the playwright? How would the real writer, if he was an aristocrat, even know Will?"

"Well, that's obvious, isn't it?" said Hamish absently. "He was involved in the production of his plays, and young Will was an actor in them. There was a big theatrical community across the Thames in Southwark, and..."

"The Bard took him under his wing... and he was so bloody gorgeous that he fell for him!" interrupted Oz excitedly. "And addressed most of the sonnets to him."

"Hang on," said Hamish, his interest caught. "What do you base that on?"

"Well, for one thing, we actually know the Lovely Boy's name. It was Will! Sonnets 135 and 136 talk of almost nothing else.

Whoever hath her wish, thou hast thy Will,
And Will to boot, and Will in overplus

There's something hovering in my mind that I can't quite

put my finger on… Never mind. I shall have to put my thinking cap on."

"Put your bonnet to its right use – tis for the head," said Hamish. "Oh, very good, my lord! Nice one."

They all laughed. One idea was chasing another, the tectonic plates of Oz's brain shifting just a fraction at lightning speed.

Olivia hadn't really been listening, but instead had been flicking through her phone. Now, she dabbed her mouth with a paper napkin.

"Changing the subject, I've got a day off tomorrow," she said. "And I'm going up to London. My brother's leaving to work in Paris, and I want to see him before he goes, to say goodbye. I've got some sartorial and financial advice to pass on, would you believe. Do you want to come with me, Ham?"

"I'd forgotten that Larry's got that new job," said Hamish. "No, I think I'll just have a quiet day. Need to keep brushing up my lines. You never know... You go and do your family thing."

"If Polly's still in hospital when I come back, we must go and see him," said Olivia. "Will you come along as well, Oz?"

But Oz had an abstracted look in his eye and didn't answer. "Oz?"

Oz stirred himself and stood up.

"Count me in. Bye, my darlings. Things to think, people to see. Simply must dash!"

In a swirl of elegant play acting he kissed both of them full on the mouth, bowed deeply, and started to make his exit, doffing an imaginary cap. All he lacked was a cloak and a cane, thought Olivia. Other actors in the cafe regarded him curiously, perhaps envying his overt theatricality.

But at the door he suddenly stopped. He turned on his heel and returned to their table, biting his lip and looking uncharacteristically serious.

"Do you know what? It's really coming together now," he said slowly. There was a faraway look in his eye. "I've totally got it. At last. You're not going to believe this. I even know why the legend of Stratford-upon-Avon didn't begin until several years after Will Shaxpur died."

He gazed at them without really seeing them, like someone recovering consciousness after a long coma.

"I've been so blind. Totally obvious. It's been staring us in the face all the time."

"Put us out of our misery, for heaven's sake," said Hamish impatiently.

"No, I'm going to go and check through the *Sonnets* again." He shook his head. "We've all been so stupid. But now I know the truth. It's all in there. You should just read 'Sonnet 81'. He could hardly have made it any clearer."

At that moment the lights in the cafe flickered and died. Startled, the other customers looked up from their *soy frappucinos* and their mobile phones, the bar staff stopped clattering crockery, the swing doors to the kitchens touched and then clung together, the cash register stilled its hum. The only sounds were from the ducks quacking on the river and the traffic on the nearby street. Daylight still streamed in through the French windows.

"Oh my God, Oz. you've done it now," said Olivia. Her face had gone white.

Oz looked round at the cafe, its silent diners staring at

him. He raised an elegant hand in farewell, stepped out into the sunlight and was gone.

Almost immediately the machines began to come on again, one by one. The life of the cafe reverted to its comforting buzz and clatter as the diners resumed their conversations. "My God," said Hamish. "He seems to be onto something." "On something, more like, knowing Oz," said Olivia, checking her handbag. "I don't like it at all. Right. I've got to dash too. Another session with Wardrobe."

She pecked Hamish on the cheek and flew back inside the theatre. But Hamish sat at the table for a long time alone, drumming his fingers, and making a mental note to look up 'Sonnet 81'.

15

"Ah, *the Players are come hither. You are welcome, masters, welcome all.* Have you left your cart outside the hospital? And you too, beautiful lady," said Polly. He pushed away his book and ran a hand through his sparse hair. "Grab yourselves some chairs from over there. I'm not meant to have more than two visitors at a time, but I don't think the nurses are too bothered. If you'd given me a bit of notice, I would have brushed my hair and changed my pyjamas."

"Never mind, Polly," said Olivia, leaning over to give him a peck on the cheek. "You look very distinguished, every inch the wounded thespian. We've brought you some grapes, obviously. Only Ham's already eaten half of them. How are you, really? You're certainly looking a lot better than when we saw you last."

Polly looked thinner, she thought, but still handsome and craggy. Tubes were running into him from a stand by the bed, and pinging noises rang out from time to time. The once familiar face from stage and film was now nearly forgotten by the public, and he had gone unrecognized by the other patients and staff on the ward.

"Better now," he said wearily, "but it hasn't been exactly a pleasant few days. I had to have my stomach pumped out, blood transfusions, God knows what. They took it very seriously, I must say. Complications, apparently. My guess is that I've caught some infection here in the hospital on top of everything else. Anyway, I'm off oysters for life, I can tell you that."

"Sorry we haven't had time to come before. Have you had a lot of visitors?" asked Olivia.

"No, strangely enough neither of my ex-wives have managed the journey. Surprise, surprise. My daughter's texted me quite a few times from Singapore though, bless her. Having the usual boyfriend trouble, needless to say. I've suggested she be *somewhat scanter of her maiden presence*."

They all laughed.

"Why do hospitals all have this particular smell? It's not exactly disinfectant. Perhaps a mixture of a lot of things," said Oz, smiling at a young male nurse who was looking after an elderly patient in the next bed. The boy smiled back. "I think I'd rather fancy being in hospital. Plenty of drama to observe, and nice young people to attend to your every whim."

Polly blew his cheeks out.

"Something like that, if you try not to think about the meals they try and force on you. 'Just had food poisoning, have we, sir? Then we prescribe congealed dog food, followed by bitter crab apple jelly with doughy pastry and thick gloopy custard with extra sugar.' Give me strength. They don't even read their own dietary advice leaflets. Do you think you could actually spare me any of those grapes, Ham? I'm starving."

"You must be getting better." Hamish guiltily handed over what was left in the brown paper bag.

"And as for sleep," Polly continued. "You're lucky if you get any at all with the racket some of those junior doctors make. They gather at that desk over there, and chatter at the top of their voices all night. It's like being next door to a party that you're not invited to. Otherwise, okay, it's no worse than boarding school was. And without the compulsory games, thank God." He looked around at his little audience. "Worst of all though, they won't let me smoke. And I don't suppose you've smuggled in a drop of vodka for me as well, have you? No, I thought not." He sighed.

"We're all missing your rants, Polly," said Hamish. "You'd better not be too long getting back though – Arnold's doing a great job as Polly. And he's still playing Gravedigger as well."

"Is he?" said Polly nervously. "I'll never hear the last of this. He's been after my part for ages. Of course, the old fool's well past it, judging by the hash he made of Friar Lawrence last season. Ha! He must be on his knees with exhaustion." He sniffed, and the others laughed. The rivalry between the two older actors was no secret in the company.

"Ah well, what have you three been up to? Waft a breath of culture over me, for God's sake."

They talked for a while in the awkward way of hospital visits, giving Polly snippets of gossip about the theatre. A family group sitting round a nearby bed tapped on their mobile phones, the patient included, no words passing between them for long minutes. Then Hamish said, "Oz has got something to tell you, Polly. This should give you something to think about in between all your medical activities."

"Well, I don't know if this is the time or place," said Oz, moving closer to the bed. "But yes, I've got something really amazing to try on you."

"Oh, no," Olivia groaned. "Not that rubbish again, pur-leeze."

"No, come on, Oz," said Hamish, squeezing Olivia's arm and smiling at her. "Let's hear it. This should be good stuff. Take it away, Oz."

"Okay," said Oz. "This is the big one. You know we said the Bard – the London guy, if you like, the real writer – must have been closely associated with the Royal Court to have all that inside knowledge, and access all the information he needed. But he had to keep his identity secret." Oz was uncharacteristically excited.

Polly nodded in agreement.

"That's my thinking, yes. The first plays were all published anonymously, probably because it was so dangerous then to express political opinions. Particularly so for an aristocrat. The Elizabethan Court was described at the time as 'a web of intrigue and jealousy', and the atmosphere was rarefied. You could be sent to the Tower for annoying the Queen, or hanged, drawn and quartered for anything they considered treason. This meant they would partly strangle you before they slowly cut…"

"Don't, Polly!" Olivia shuddered and closed her eyes. "I don't want to know!"

"All right. But a dreadful death, and a good enough reason to stay anonymous, I reckon."

"Exactly," said Oz. "And the Bard would have been involved in that world on the south bank of the Thames right up to his neck. That's where the theatres, taverns and brothels were – and the actors. Including a particularly beautiful young actor from Stratford-upon-Avon, one Will Shaxpur."

"*Ta da!*" said Hamish. "Enter our local hero!"

"Yes, so what happens? The Bard falls for him, head over heels. Utterly infatuated. So much so that nearly all the sonnets are addressed to him, many of them mentioning his name, which we know without question to be Will."

Polly said, "Hmm. Yes, I think I see where you're coming from. Go on."

"So there comes a time around 1593 when the Bard needs to put a name to his plays and poetry. As you say, the first fifteen plays were anonymous. But by now they are so successful and popular, they have to be *by* somebody. The writer can't use his own name. So what does he do?"

Oz leant forward, his face tense. You could have heard a surgical needle drop.

"He pays the sweet boy the biggest compliment he conceivably can. He takes *his* name, adapts it very slightly, and from then on signs his plays *William Shake-speare,* in homage to the boy. With a hyphen. Much more poetic than plain Will Shaxpur, of course, but a nice romantic sort of name, and close enough. And presumably nothing like the writer's own name, whatever that may have been. It's blindingly obvious when you think of it."

16

Your name from hence immortal life shall have,
Though I, once gone, to all the world must die
Sonnet 81

Oz's face was radiating with an excitement the others were beginning to share. His enthusiasm was infectious. Polly sat up a little against his pillows, stifling a groan. Hamish nodded.

"It makes sense, you know, Polly, the more you think about it. I knew that the hyphen in a name was often used to denote a pseudonym. But is there any evidence for it? In his writings perhaps?"

"Yes! There is indeed. That's the beauty of it!" said Oz loudly, punching the air. A little group of visitors at another bed looked around curiously, and a pretty nurse taking someone's blood pressure raised her head.

"It's all through the sonnets, staring at us. Sonnets 55, 76, and 81. '*Your name from hence immortal life shall have...*' and 95, '*The beauty of thy budding name*'. Then comes the clincher in 108. '*E'en as when first I hallowed thy fair name*.' He's taken his name and made it holy! He could hardly have spelt it out any more clearly. And yet everyone's missed it."

They all looked serious, thinking about what Oz had said.

Olivia was the first to speak.

"For goodness' sake, how can it be that nobody else has seen it if it's so obvious? All those thousands of books about the 'Shakespeare Secret', but they have never spotted that one?"

"Polly? What do you say?" Oz looked at Polly, who shrugged. Two red spots had appeared on his pale cheeks and his eyes were bright. "Who knows? Possibly the idea is so radical that it got suppressed. Treading on too many toes perhaps."

"But do you believe it? Is it valid?"

Polly blew out a long puff of air.

"I don't know yet. I'll have to think about it. Check out the dates, for one thing. Was young Shaxpur working at the Globe Theatre as an actor at the time the pseudonym first appeared? Was he in London when the sonnets were written? Actually, come to think of it, I'm pretty sure he was." He screwed up his face in concentration. "I'll grant you, as a hypothesis, it's got legs. Let me just think this out. Okay, let's test your theory – and it is only a theory – a stage further. Try this. Will loves the idea of his name being used but has been sworn to secrecy on the subject. Just like Hamlet swears his friends to silence about seeing the Ghost."

"Oh yes!" said Hamish. "Hamlet makes a big thing of it. *'Swear...nay, but swear it! Upon my sword...'*"

Some of the visitors to the bedsides looked up, curious to hear this spirited conversation. One woman had recognized Olivia and was whispering excitedly to her companion.

"Yes, all right. That's the bit," said Polly, irritated at having his train of thought interrupted. "So as an inducement to keep quiet and never reveal the identity of the real author,

Will is given a whacking big payoff, including the finance to buy shares in the theatre company. This would explain how he could afford to do that on an actor's meagre pay."

A young woman came past each bed with a trolley offering Mars bars, chocolates, crisps and other delicacies apparently essential to the healing process. Hamish smiled at her. Polish, he decided. Or perhaps Bulgarian. Blonde anyway. She was frowning at the coffee dispenser, banging it and tutting. Polly waved the trolley on.

"There's another thing," said Oz. "Before long, the Bard, or more likely the Royal Court, have had enough of young Will's indiscreet nature. So what do they do? They stop his mouth with more gold. In other words, they buy him off. He is packed off back to Stratford with an enormous bribe, large enough for him to buy pretty well the biggest house in his home town, on condition that he stays up there and keeps his mouth shut. And in 1597 he goes home and does just that. So this addresses that crucial question, often raised, never properly answered before. How on earth could Willie Shaxpur, a mere jobbing actor who'd been in London less than ten years, afford to buy New Place, a large house with twenty rooms, and other areas of land? But now we know, don't we?"

Oz was more relaxed now that he had made his big reveal to Polly. He settled back in the chair stroking his cheek, a smile playing over his handsome face. Hamish absent-mindedly reached across the bed to finish off the last few grapes. He leant forward and crumpled up the bag.

"Yes, I get it too. I must say the Lovely Boy idea makes a lot more sense than the ludicrous concept that the

Bard wrote the plays in his spare time after a long day's acting. So young Will starts bragging in his cups to the other actors. 'Yes, *I* wrote all those plays, you know.'" He thought for a moment. "Maybe he even tries his hand at a bit of writing himself. People don't like it. And this, of course, is where various strange comments come in. *'He hath small Latin, and less Greek,'* said Ben Jonson. Well, that would be true enough. *'Yes, I wish he had blotted ev'ry line.'* No one could possibly have said that of the true Shakespeare. Hey, they were talking about Will's own poor efforts."

"Yes," said Oz. "Well spotted, Ham. And Robert Greene, fellow actor and a playwright, calls him an *'upstart crow'*, the cheeky little madam. A strange way indeed to describe the great Shakespeare, while 'upstart crow' could indeed describe young Willie – who was getting well up himself by this time. God, tell me about it. I know that type so well." He turned away, tilting his head and half closing his eyes.

Hamish was doing a little dance, turning into Professor Higgins in *My Fair Lady*.

"I think he's got it! By George, he's got it! The rain in Spain stays mainly in the plain…"

Olivia sighed and turned her head away, tucking in Polly's sheet and plumping up his pillows for him. Polly, so far, had said nothing more.

"Shut up, Ham. This is big," said Oz. "We have just one personal observation on record about the Stratford man. Do you know how John Aubrey described him? *'A handsome, well-shaped man, very good company, and of a ready and smooth wit.'* It's virtually the only eyewitness description of Shaxpur that we have. The *only* one. Pure gold. '*A handsome, well-shaped man*', eh? That sounds exactly like the young man the Bard might have fallen for so heavily, don't you think? Someone of exceptional beauty, although no longer a boy exactly of course." Oz had a big grin on his face. "Looks as if you like my theory, guys. What sayst thou now, Sir Polly?"

Polly raised a hand above the bedclothes and paused before he spoke.

"I say, okay, but hold on a bit. Let's not get carried away. I'm certainly not committing myself yet. Yes, I can't deny I'm intrigued. But I'd like to do a lot of research before we all get ahead of ourselves."

Olivia took his hand, looking worried.

"Look, Polly. You've had a pretty sharp warning not to interfere in all this, haven't you? I keep telling you all, you're playing with fire."

Polly smiled and squeezed her hand back.

"Fair enough, Ol. I've learnt my lesson. Don't count too much on me, you two. Doesn't mean I'm not going to keep studying it, though. It's too fascinating to let it go entirely. '*Hallowed thy fair name*', you said? Well, if your idea is right, he certainly did that." Olivia groaned and sat back down, defeated.

17

There was activity everywhere as hospital staff bustled around the ward. The shifts had changed and routine procedures had clanked into action. Visiting time was over, without the need for any overt announcements. A nurse was approaching Polly's bedside with a large folder under her arm. She was overweight, and pushing a wheeled machine seemed an effort.

The three actors stirred and prepared their farewells. Hamish had a thoughtful look on his face.

"There are a hell of a lot of implications to this," he said. "I'm going to make some notes. First of all – yes, of course, it would explain an awful lot about our man in Stratford. A much more rational scenario. He was an actor in London who went home and busied himself buying land, leaving his city life behind him, except for occasional visits. Secondly, it's obvious now why he didn't leave any books, notes, manuscripts, or documents of any sort in his will.

'*Whoever hath her wish, thou hast thy Will,*
    And Will to boot, and Will in overplus.''

"Because he wasn't a writer at all. Or, perhaps just a dabbler."

"Spot on, Oz. He may also have been involved in peddling

various plays around the theatre world, and getting involved in producing. There is some evidence for that. He was also a shareholder in the theatre company. But as for being the great writer – no way."

The nurse's presence was moving them away from the bedside.

"I'll just take your blood pressure," she said cheerfully to Polly. "Let's pop this on your arm. Do you know your date of birth? Pop these pills in for me. They'll help to relax you. Are you allergic to anything? Now, have you opened your bowels today at all?"

"Do you want me to pop open my bowels for you right now?" growled Polly. "And you should know my date of birth by heart by now – I've told you enough times already. I don't hold with all these drugs. If I pop anything else, I'll burst."

The nurse laughed.

"Having another grumpy day, Polly? Shall I get you a nice strong laxative? It's no trouble. We're just trying to keep you alive, you know."

Polly was about to reply when Hamish cut in quickly.

"Bye, Polly," he said. "I can see you're in capable hands. See you again soon. Plenty for us all to think about." He hesitated. "There's another massive question, isn't there? Another even bigger elephant in the room. If Willy Shaxpur didn't write the plays… er, well, who did?"

"That's your department, Ham." Polly waved his hand dismissively. The nurse puffed with effort as she struggled with the machine. She muttered, "This thing isn't working very well today. It's started playing up again."

"Hm. This is really beginning to intrigue me, you know," said Hamish. "The Bard was obviously a man with an amazing education and the means to devote himself to writing. Intimately familiar with life at Court, in this country and abroad. And had spent a helluva lot of time in Italy, by the sound of it. I wonder if…"

But Polly was no longer listening, so Olivia grabbed Hamish's arm.

"That's quite enough of that. Come on, all of you, time we weren't here."

"Yes, we're just popping off now," Hamish leered. The nurse was staring at the reading on the monitor and shaking her head. The three friends looked at each other. and silently agreed that this was the perfect moment for them to tiptoe away. They clattered down the long wide hospital staircase and out into the fresh air with an obvious sense of relief.

They skirted the clump of bushes at the edge of the precinct, where a little group of people were dragging furiously on cigarettes. Hamish thought he spotted blue hospital uniforms among them and muttered something to Olivia. She ignored him. The conversation grew more animated as the three went into the multi-storey car park. Their voices rang through the large echoing space.

"What do you reckon, is there something in it, then?"

"I can somehow imagine him taking the boy's name, I'll grant you that."

"But how else did he afford to buy the biggest house in Stratford if he wasn't the playwright? Because he was bought off."

"Well, if he didn't write the plays, who did? Answer me that."

"Why do these places always smell of pee?"

"It's all pure speculation. Load of rubbish. You want to know who wrote Shakespeare? Shakespeare did."

"Ha ha. Very funny. Have either of you actually read all the sonnets, sweethearts? No, thought not."

"Whole thing makes perfect sense to me anyway. Where would he have suddenly gained all that knowledge?"

"Yes, it would have taken years. Since early childhood."

"I don't really care who wrote them anyway. What does it matter?"

"By the way, let's keep all this to ourselves, shall we? I don't think our colleagues will be very sympathetic, do you? All agreed?"

"No, agreed. Mum's the word."

"Polly's getting marvellous treatment. Shame he's always so grumpy."

"Listen, can anyone remember which floor we parked on?"

"Yeah, well, I'm starving."

"It was over by the lifts, I remember that. God, this place stinks."

"Here we are. Anybody got change for the machine?"

"Hospitals always make me hungry. Shall we stop off and get some fish and chips on the way?"

This final proposition met with unanimous approval.

18

When I perhaps compounded am with clay
Do not so much as my poor name rehearse
Sonnet 71

Now the visitors had gone, the ward settled back into its afternoon torpor. Most of the patients were dozing in the heat. A fly was buzzing against a windowpane offering a restricted view of a row of regimented flower beds. Polly could see a cloud of midges above them, dancing in the sunlight. The nurses had now all disappeared from the scene. Apart from the faint clicking sounds of electronic music in someone's earphones, the ward was silent.

Polly lay back on his freshly plumped up pillows. Oz had certainly given him a lot to think about with his astonishing revelation. So the playwright had assumed as his pseudonym the name of his fair youth, the handsome Will Shaxpur from Stratford. He had to admit now he thought of it, that it made perfect sense. Changing the ugly name Shaxpur or Shaxper to the much more stylish *William Shake-speare* was a logical step, and the ultimate accolade the Bard could pay to the object of his love. '*Your name from hence immortal life shall have*' said it as plain as a pikestaff.

If the writer were an aristocrat, he would have had to conceal his identity. It was unthinkable – even unlawful –

for a noble to admit to having a paid occupation. Not only that, the highly controversial ideas expressed in some of the plays would have been politically very dangerous. He must have had a lot of influence to survive with his head still on his shoulders.

Nothing was said about him in his lifetime either. No encounters, no mentions, no letters or notes or books. Beyond weird. Plenty known about de Vere as such, and a little about Shakespeare as a businessman in faraway Stratford. But of 'William Shake-speare, writer and poet' - a total void. Mark Twain wrote under a pseudonym too, his real name was Samuel Clemens. Ditto John le Carre, George Eliot, Moliere, George Orwell, Lewis Carroll, many others, all pen names. It is hardly unusual for a writer to be anonymous. But for them not to be feted when they died is unheard of.

So the Royal Court must have known who he was. Of course, Elizabeth herself was far from a fool. She was taught from an early age by tutors from Cambridge University. She spoke several foreign languages, and had studied Latin and Greek. She would have taken a keen interest in the plays and known who the writer really was. She must have instructed that the true identity of the writer be kept secret, on pain of torture or death. Why she was so protective of him, Polly could only guess.

She would have used an agent though. Someone the Court trusted to handle the delicate matter of the writer's anonymity. A ruthless man of action, with literary connections perhaps? There was someone who fitted those criteria in the back of his mind... if only he could remember.

Polly shrugged. He was drowsier now as the drugs took

effect. Nice of those young people to have come to see him. His own children were far away in Australia and Singapore, of course. As for his former wives, the activities of divorce lawyers had put paid to any reconciliation in either case. He groaned and turned his head on the pillow. This was familiar territory, all the more painful for never being far from his mind even after all these years. Better to return to the Elizabethan court of the late sixteenth century. Who was behind the Stratford myth? Someone must have masterminded a cover story for the writer.

Of course! He almost sat up in bed, but was restrained by the tight blanket and the tube running into his wrist. Ben Jonson was the obvious candidate for the job! Twice killed a man, been branded on the thumb for being a felon, yet was a leading playwright himself, and still unaccountably very much in favour with the Queen. What better choice of someone to pay off young Shaxpur for them.

And twenty years later, when the First Folio was being assembled, Jonson was the perfect agent to deal with the now prosperous man of property who had become a blabbering drunkard. Then later, he would set up a tomb and begin to create the legend of the Swan of Avon…

With the publication of the Folio, people would soon be starting to question who this 'William Shake-speare' was, the man whose name was appended to them. Now that the Bard and Shaxpur were both safely dead, it would have seemed prudent to create the impression that the man from Stratford had been the writer. And so the legend was born.

It was all becoming clear now, so clear, so clear. This was exciting stuff. But bearing in mind Olivia's nonsense about the Shadow, he'd keep a low profile. With a smile of satisfaction on his gnarled face, as the quiet life of the hospital ward ebbed and flowed around him, Polly fell asleep.

19

Hamish woke up early after the visit to the hospital the previous day. He too felt excited. Oz's revelations about the identification of young Will, the handsome actor from Stratford, as being the adored subject of many of the sonnets, seemed entirely convincing. So did the adoption of his name by the Bard as his *nom de plume* for his writings.

And so, Hamish thought, as he stood by the washbasin cleaning his teeth, it invited the next question. If TB was not the man from Warwickshire, then who was the real Bard? Was it de Vere, as Polly was so sure? It was time to find out. And he had the leisure to do so.

He glanced at Olivia's fair head as she lay sleeping in their bed, one suntanned arm lying on top of the duvet. God, she was gorgeous. He moved over to the bed and looked down at her. What was this emotion he felt? Desire certainly. But tenderness too, and a deep concern for her wellbeing. Could this be love? He frowned in perplexity at this unfamiliar feeling. As he did so, Olivia stirred and opened her eyes. She smiled up at him and reached out a hand to take his.

"Hello! You're up early. Have we anything to do today…? What time is it?"

She got out of bed naked and brushed past him on her way to the bathroom. Her back had tiny creases in it from the way she had been lying.

"I almost forgot! I'm going to Birmingham this morning to do an interview. This is ridiculous. I've got a brain like a sieve." She slammed the bathroom door behind her and continued the conversation through it.

"You didn't mention that last night?" called Hamish, pulling on a towelling robe and getting back into bed. He pulled his laptop towards him from where it had been charging at the bedside. "What's the rush?"

"No big rush really, but it's time I moved. Tell you when I've had my shower," came the muffled reply, followed by the sound of the toilet flushing and the shower being turned on. Hamish sighed and opened his laptop.

The claim of the Stratford man to the position had been questioned by countless commentators over the years. There were many candidates for the role of the Bard. The list included Sir Francis Bacon, the Earl of Derby, Christopher Marlowe, and even Queen Elizabeth herself. More recent contenders were Henry Neville and William Hastings. But always the front runner was Polly's favourite, the shadowy figure of Edward de Vere. He checked his notes.

Edward de Vere, 17th Earl of Oxford. Born 12th April 1550, died 24th June 1604. He was a royal

Ward of Court. He went to both Queens College, Oxford, and St Johns College, Cambridge. Studied law at Gray's Inn in 1567.

The Earl's familiar environment was a Royal Court, including those in France and Italy. That would explain why virtually all the plays in the canon take place in such settings. De Vere was steeped in philosophy, classical literature, and the law, and was extremely well read. Even more convincingly, de Vere was devoted to literary pursuits, particularly the theatre, and he was known as a promising poet. However, his own poems were never seen again once the works later attributed to Shakespeare began to appear. That was highly significant.

De Vere was also an enthusiastic traveller, and in 1575 he set out on a long visit to Europe. Such a journey was later to become the custom for wealthy aristocrats, known as the Grand Tour. De Vere was immensely taken with Italy and stayed there for over a year. He was known as being interested in Italian fashion, and was a bit of a dandy.

Hamish already knew that no less than thirteen of the plays were set in Italy. What also intrigued him was the wealth of detail about de Vere's life that fitted in with what was revealed about the playwright from his works. Like Hamlet, he wooed the Lord Chancellor's daughter, and was in a ship that was captured by pirates, and like King Lear, he had three daughters himself. There were many other events in his life with echoes in the plays.

Above all, de Vere's lifestyle gave him the leisure to study and write, without the necessity of earning a living. He would also have had access to university libraries, and to the relatively small stock of books in Tudor London. His tutor had an extensive private library.

Hamish read on, his attention totally held. The sonnets were written between 1590 and 1604, stopping just before de Vere's death at the age of fifty-four. In 'Sonnet 73', the poet is an old man musing on his approaching death. Yet Will Shaxpur was only in his thirties when it was composed, making it implausible that he wrote the sonnets.

There were also intriguing hints as to de Vere's name hidden in the plays and the sonnets themselves. Interested scholars have paid a lot of attention to occurrences of the word 'very,' where it might be seen to represent the name de Vere. Curiouser and curiouser, thought Hamish, in the words of *Alice in Wonderland*.

Hamish extracted himself with an effort from the late sixteenth century to become aware of Olivia glancing at herself in the full-length wardrobe mirror. For someone who didn't seem vain or self-obsessed, she certainly paid a lot of attention to her appearance. She was making some minute adjustment to the suit she had bought in Harrods' Sale last season. Hamish knew she hadn't previously found an occasion to wear the suit.

The bed was now spread with books, a notebook, and his laptop. He shook his head in disbelief.

"This man de Vere is amazing. Polly was right. Reading about him reveals so many things about Shakespeare's identity that suddenly make sense. You can see the events of the plays coming through his life. Such a contrast with poor old Shaxpur. Quite a relief, frankly."

Olivia gave her outfit a final brush down with her hand and leant over the bed.

"I've no idea what you're talking about, darling, but mind that pen on the duvet. The ink will never come out. Got to go now… Wish me luck. I'll be back in time for supper, unless anything crops up."

She looked every inch the successful actress as they kissed. He was abashed and felt obliged to take an interest in her day. "What is this thing exactly? Some big deal?"

"No, it's just a regional television arts programme. We're being interviewed to promote the play. Bookings aren't too hot at the moment as you very well know, and this is somebody's bright idea to help beat the drum." She glanced at the large watch on her wrist. "We've got to be at the studios by midday. I think it's where Pebble Mill used to be before they pulled it down."

Hamish was suddenly seized with guilt and pushed away his papers. "Look, are you sure you don't want me to run you to the station? I can throw some clothes on in a second."

"No, it's fine. I told you, the Sir's going as well, and he's actually condescended to give me a lift in his chauffeur-driven Merc. No mere trains for him. Should be here at any moment."

"You're travelling with that creep? You didn't tell me he was going too!"

"Yes, I did. You just don't listen, that's all." She peered through the window to look onto the road, where a large shiny car with darkened windows was parked outside the flat. A figure was just discernible in the back. "Oh Lord, he's here already. He's early, wouldn't you just know it? Got to dash."

And with that she fled. It was Hamish's turn now to twitch the curtains, in time to see the rear door of the car being opened for her. He raised a hand in farewell, but she was already in animated conversation with the unseen passenger and didn't look up. The car drove smoothly away and disappeared.

20

**What should such fellows as I do crawling between earth and heaven?
We are arrant knaves, all.**
Act III, scene i

After Olivia had gone, Hamish turned again to de Vere, following up various references to other websites. There were a couple more books he needed to get from the Shakespeare Institute too, but for the moment there was plenty to go at online.

The huge problems about the identification of Will Shaxpur as the writer – his lack of a classical education, any opportunity to be familiar with the Royal Courts of Europe, no indication of travel to Italy, and countless other deficiencies in his biography - simply did not apply to Edward de Vere. But his identification as the playwright was kept a secret so tightly that it was still being maintained four hundred years after his death. The Queen must have known who he was, Hamish mused. And so did the King who succeeded her. James I even increased the large pension Elizabeth had awarded de Vere.

"A thousand pounds a year? Why would they give him that?" he asked aloud, chewing the end of his felt pen. That was an enormous income at that time. There must have been a very powerful reason for it. Neither the Queen nor James were exactly famed for their generosity. Had they been trying to hide something? When de Vere died in 1604 there was no mention of even a funeral. Why then was there no public acclaim at his death, let alone his burial in Westminster Abbey as would normally be obligatory for a senior Earl? Yet James had referred to de Vere as 'great Oxford'. Mystery on mystery. Hamish sighed. Enough of all this.

He pushed his laptop and books aside, stretched, and got out of bed. It was high time he put some clothes on. His studious mood was broken, his interest in Edward de Vere temporarily lost. He felt childishly sulky that Olivia was going to Birmingham to be interviewed on television, while he, a mere understudy, was totally ignored. It was hard to shake off this feeling of depression while he was showering and towelling himself dry. It had persisted all the time he worked on de Vere. He knew he was subject to what Churchill had called the Black Dog, and he felt powerless to cope with it. It was in his genes. It was like a shadow falling across his life.

He suddenly recollected Olivia's contention that the Shadow of Shakespeare - presumably the real writer - was still roaming the nether world like the ghost of Hamlet's father. She maintained the Shadow was actively upset about people poking their noses into the secret of its creator's real identity. What absolute rubbish. He groaned aloud with frustration. These thoughts reverberated through his head, often repeating themselves, until he could scream.

What the hell am I doing, hanging around this town with virtually nothing to do, while everybody else in the theatre seems to be having a great time? Am I really any good as an actor?

Who says I am? If I was, I'd be up there on the stage every night instead of twiddling my thumbs waiting for the bloody Sir to catch flu. Pity he doesn't fall under a bus. Not that he'd know what a bus was.

Hamish stared at himself in the mirror, lines from the play running through his brain. *'Who calls me villain? Breaks my pate across? Yet I, a dull and muddy-mettled rascal, peak like John-a-dreams, unpregnant of my cause.'* And she's gone off with the Sir to a television studio, no doubt to wine and dine with him afterwards in some super-duper restaurant. What did Olivia mean when she said she'd be back unless something 'cropped up'? Hamish shook his head in anger at himself. It's lucky the Sir is gay, he thought. Otherwise there was no limit to what he might be imagining in the mood he was in.

'I am very proud, revengeful, ambitious, with more offences at my beck than I have thoughts to put them in, imagination to give them shape, or time to act them in.'

I wonder what Ol really feels about me? Does she want to be saddled with a failure like me? She could snap her fingers and have any man she wanted. Why on earth should she bother with me? Anyway, all that aside – what am I going to do with my life? If I can't make it as an actor, I'm going to have to look for an alternative career. Chartered accountant? Lawyer? Doctor? Teacher?

He groaned aloud at the prospect. Anyway, it was far too late to start studying for a profession. If he couldn't stomach the idea of an orthodox career, what then? Run a restaurant? Become an IT computer boffin? Work for a local authority? Join the Navy?

Sometimes I wonder why I go on at all. Why do any of us? What's the point of it all, when you come to think of it?

'*To die, to sleep. To sleep, perchance to dream. Ay, there's the rub…*'

He looked out the window. It was a lovely day with not a cloud in the sky. Somehow that only made him feel worse. This wouldn't do. He'd have to get out for some fresh air. He pulled on a pair of trainers and slammed the door behind him.

I know what I'll do, he decided as he walked. I'll give myself twelve months to make it as an actor, and not as just a bloody understudy. If it isn't happening by then, I'll find another career or die in the attempt. That's it. Cracked it. One year from now.

His step was lighter as he approached the town centre. Make a decision and stick to it, that was the secret. He looked up at the sky. There you are, the sun's still shining.

The sooner I get to the Duck and sink a pint of Hooky, the better. I wonder how Ol's getting on with her television interview. Nobody's going to interview me, that's for sure. What's it like being an understudy? Do tell our fascinated viewers. They can't wait to hear how wonderful your life is. Ha ha.

Perhaps I actually could be a teacher, when you come to think of it. At least I do have a degree, even if it is only a 2:2. That was a pretty poor deal too. If only I'd spent more time swotting up instead of playing football and chasing girls…

He sighed again. It looked like it was going to be a long day till Ol got home. If she hadn't run off with the Sir, that was.

21

**Whoever hath her wish, thou hast thy Will
And Will to boot, and Will in overplus**
Sonnet 135

"It's all here," said Oz to himself, shaking his head in wonder as he reached the theatre. He pushed the well-thumbed *Sonnets* back into his shoulder bag and went out on to the terrace. It was another sunny day, with little white clouds scudding across the sky far above him, and a gentle breeze rustling the trees by the river.

"Think of 'Sonnet 81'. What could be clearer? He is telling the young man, '*Your name from hence immortal life shall have, Though I once gone to all the world must die.*' And he knew his verse was immortal. Just fantastic. It's all laid out here in the *Sonnets* for anyone to read."

"Hello, Oz. Steady on, calm down."

"Hi, Ham! Hi, Polly. Sorry, just muttering to myself. How's it going? How did Ol get on in Birmingham with the Sir yesterday?"

"It went fine, I think. Hardly seen her this morning. But they got some good PR for the play, I think, " said Hamish. "I haven't had time to watch the recording of it yet. Ol would have been brilliant as usual though, I guarantee that."

"We certainly need some good PR, darling." Oz turned

to Polly. The older man was leaning on the terrace railing with Hamish. "Good to see you back, Polly. You're going on tonight, I hear. You must be much better?"

"Yes, I bloody well am," said Polly, drawing furiously on his cigarette. "They couldn't find anything more to do to me, so I discharged myself from the place before I caught something else. Anyway, I couldn't bear the thought of that old fool Arnold doing my part a minute longer. The thing's not meant to be a bloody comedy. No wonder Hamlet murdered him behind the arras."

Oz privately thought Polly should be very grateful for the medical treatment he had received from NHS staff who were hardworking and even harder pressed by an over -bureaucratic system, but held back from starting an argument.

"Let's stay here for a bit, shall we? We've got half an hour. I want to talk about the sonnets."

They found a table where they could look right down the river and sat down. It was a busy scene, and the sun had brought a lot of people to the riverside area near the huge theatre building. Oz sipped a cappuccino and began to unwrap a tuna mayonnaise sandwich he'd brought with him. Hamish had a Becks, which he was drinking straight from the bottle. Polly lit another cigarette, squinting against the bright sunlight.

"Go on, let's hear what you've dug up."

"Right. First of all, let's look at the Sweet Boy. His name is Will, which is constantly mentioned throughout the sonnets. The word Will occurs thirteen times in 'Sonnet 135' alone! But now at last we can understand why." Oz was glancing down at his phone, where he had recorded his notes.

"And in 'Sonnet 136', the Bard exults in his new pseudonym, because he is now also called Will, like his beloved. *'Make but my name thy love, and love that still, And then thou lov'st me, for my name is Will.'* I'm Will too now, he is saying to the young man." He smiled and looked round at the others on the terrace.

"Hi, there!" Oz was obviously enjoying being the centre of attention, and frequently exchanged greetings with passers-by. He continued his theme. "And here's another one. *'The beauty of thy budding name'*... and then later, *'Naming thy name. My name be buried where my body is!'* It all makes perfect sense. TB will lose his own name, which will be buried with him."

Below the terrace, a pair of Canada geese executed a noisy landing on the river, screeching to a halt like a plane overshooting the runway. They glared round indignantly at the spectators as if to reproach them for their smiles. Polly and Hamish turned back and resumed listening to Oz.

"Right, ready for the clincher? He actually spells it out specifically in 'Sonnet 108', the poem that has the lovely line, *'Nothing, sweet boy'.* He says, *'Thou mine, I thine, e'en as when first I hallowed thy fair name.'* Could it be any more specific? He hallowed the boy's name by adopting it! Forgive me if I'm repeating myself from the other day."

"Hallowed?" said Hamish, screwing up his nose. "Oh yes – made holy."

"Okay – what else could all this possibly mean apart from the obvious? Anybody? Polly?"

Polly left a long silence, inspecting the ash on his cigarette in concentration.

"I will admit your theory is tempting. The scenario answers a lot of niggling doubts that have always worried scholars. Your basic theory, that the writer had simply adopted the name of his beloved Will Shaxpur, Shagsper, Shakspere, what you will - ha! - to create his pseudonym of William Shake-speare, strikes me as plausible. I have no problem with that at all, and I can't think why I never spotted it before."

Oz smiled smugly.

"You and everybody else, it seems. Just little me."

"And the dates fit pretty well, given that we don't know exactly when any of the plays were written. Our information on that is very vague. So – congratulations!"

A smirk of satisfaction lit up Oz's face.

"Yessss! I knew it. My big payday then!" His voice had gone squeaky. A few heads on the terrace turned towards them. "Just you wait till I spring this on the world! *The Shakespeare secret solved!* And what a fantastic boost for the gay cause. The Bard was gay! And he took his gay lover's name and gave him immortality." He went into a little jig. "Interviews on breakfast television… I wonder what you wear at that time in the morning. Something a bit rumpled, I think. But very expensive. And a new scarf, of course. I shall look modest and gulp a lot. They'll like that."

"Don't you dare!" said Polly, real alarm in his voice. "You've no idea the can of worms you'll be opening. The wrath of the literary world will descend on you. You can count me out for support, that's for sure. I've had my warning. I don't mind being used as a sounding board, as long as you don't expect me to do anything about it."

"Me too, Oz," said Hamish. "That's about where I'm at. On the other hand, I've been finding out some amazing facts about who..."

"Not now, Ham!" said Oz hastily. "Anyway, you can calm down, dears. I'm only pulling your legs."

But Hamish noticed he didn't meet their eyes as he said it.

22

Murder most foul, as in the best it is
Act I, scene v

"You'd better be joking," said Polly, tapping his packet of cigarettes before extracting one with his long fingers. "I'm just playing along with your idea for the sake of it, all right? Your theory is not without its snags, anyway. It doesn't answer the question, what – or rather who – was behind the big promotion of Stratford-upon-Avon as the home of the playwright after his death."

Oz shrugged.

"Well, people would have been asking who the Bard really was, obviously. So Stratford came into play, all ready to be set up."

"I've got a few ideas on that!" Hamish piped up. "It's pretty obvious who the real Bard was…"

Polly interrupted him with a wave of his hand.

"Ham, not now, all right? Let's deal with one thing at a time, shall we? You see, going along with your scenario for the moment, Oz… yes, Queen Elizabeth and later King James' court would have to have been heavily involved. They'd have been determined from the beginning to hide the real identity of the playwright, for reasons we can only guess at, some obvious, some less so. Now they needed a cover story. And a fixer. And I've a pretty good idea who that might have been."

"Mr. Fix It? Who?" asked Oz. He was serious now. "I'm all ears – do tell!"

Polly leaned back, his fingers tapping the wooden table.

"Master Ben Jonson, that's who. He crops up again and again. You know about Jonson, Oz?"

"Yes, but it's a while ago now since I came across him when I had a part in *Volpone*. Let's ask our resident Eng. Lit. honours graduate. Ham?"

"Jonson? Well, fellow playwright and poet, friend of the Bard, thought to be a strong candidate for being the Rival Poet mentioned in the *Sonnets*," Hamish said. "Wrote that line describing Shakespeare as the 'Sweet Swan of Avon', didn't he?"

"He did. And that one oblique reference is the cornerstone of the case for Shaxpur of Stratford being the playwright. It appeared in a poem Jonson wrote in that crucial year 1623, seven years after Will's death. Until then, nobody had ever mentioned the playwright having any connection with Stratford-upon-Avon. Nothing at all. As I've said before."

"That really is weird, isn't it?" said Hamish. "No, Polly, I don't know much about Jonson's life, to be honest."

"Oh, he was quite a guy. Joined the army as a youngster and served in Holland, where he killed a man. Then in 1597 he was imprisoned for sedition. A year after he was released, then he got into a duel with an actor, and killed him. He was charged with murder, and got off, but he was branded on the thumb as a felon."

"Ouch," said Hamish. "Ruthless bastard by the sound of it. But a very good writer? *Volpone* and all that."

"Certainly was. And he was the Bard's greatest fan. '*I loved the man*', he said. And surprisingly enough, he got back in with the court in spite of his record for violence, and became a real favourite of both Queen Elizabeth and of James I."

"Mr. Fix It then?" said Oz.

Polly held his hands in the air, screwing his eyes up against the smoke from his cigarette.

"I've no proof. I'm just speculating. But here's a strange thing. Jonson was awarded a substantial pension by the queen of *a hundred marks a year* as a sort of early Poet Laureate, or ostensibly so. That was a hell of a lot of money, perhaps ten times the average annual wage, and when King James came to the throne, he actually increased it."

"Jonson's reward for helping to conceal the Bard's identity then? Pretty generous."

"I'd argue he must have done a bit more than that for his money."

"I know. But go on. So what did he do?"

"Something pretty big."

Polly threw his cigarette end over the railing into the river, making Oz wince. This time the ducks ignored it, being busy further along the bank. He could see an old lady in a long shabby coat spooning bread into the water. She was as impassive as a Las Vegas gambling addict feeding a one-armed bandit without any real hope of reward. The birds quacked their noisy appreciation. A buzzer sounded on the terrace, alerting those concerned that rehearsals were about to begin.

"I think he was a hit man," Polly said quietly. "I think he was told to murder Will Shaxpur, to keep his mouth shut.

And I know how he did it."

23

Unless you would devise some virtuous lie...
My name be buried where my body is.
Sonnet 72

The three men walked into the rehearsal room and sat down. The other actors were talking quietly together while the director went over the script. Hamish turned to Polly. "What did you mean, Ben Jonson murdered him?" he said incredulously.

Polly drew closer.

"The Bard had been dead for some time when Will started boasting even more to his friends in London, where he had now bought a share in another theatre property. He'd obviously got rich and cocky and was threatening to reveal the Bard's real name. So Jonson and his fellow playwright Michael Drayton were told to silence him."

"Told by whom?"

"Well, the Royal Court is never far out of the picture. Anyway, the two men made the arduous journey up from London to Stratford and took Will out for a boozy evening. They had a wild night, according to the diary of the vicar of Stratford-upon-Avon some forty years later, the Rev. John Ward. The pub was in Bidford-on-Avon, where the river is crossed by a medieval stone bridge."

"I know the place," said Hamish. "Another nice pub there now."

"Well, legend says Will slept off his drunken evening under the pillars of that bridge, allegedly caught a fever, and died, aged just fifty-two. Buried the following week, unnoticed and unremarked by the world." Polly cleared his throat. "And that would have been that. Except that seven years later, the same Ben Jonson had a hand in editing the First Folio along with Heminges and Condell. And thank God he did, for otherwise many of the works of Shakespeare might have been lost."

Hamish whistled.

"My God. That's right. Good old Ben."

"Good old Ben indeed. At the same time, as an introduction to the Folio, he wrote a fulsome poem to the memory of the Bard. In it appears the infamous 'Sweet Swan of Avon' line. The poem begins: '*To draw no envy, Shakespeare, on thy name, Am I thus ample to thy book and fame.*' Later on he says: '*Thou art a monument without a tomb.*' The name thing again, implying there was no tomb at Holy Trinity Church at that time."

"Very intriguing," said Hamish." So you really think he bumped off poor Willie?"

"Yes, I do, actually. And here's something Jonson wrote about Will Shaxpur in 1630: '*He was, indeed, honest and of an open and free nature, had an excellent phantasy, brave notions and gentle expressions, wherein he flowed with that facility that sometimes it was necessary he should be stopped.*' And stop him, he did!"

Hamish's eyes were wide open.

"My God! You've got something there, Polly. But don't you

think he's talking about the Bard?"

"No, he's talking about young Shaxpur, who was a lovely guy, a bit of a dreamer and a fantasist, but whose garrulity spelled trouble for the vital anonymity of the real writer. Incidentally, the Rev. John Ward I mentioned earlier, was dismayed to find that, of course, Shakespeare was not remembered as a writer at all. He wrote in 1668:

> 'I have heard that Mr Shakspeare was a natural wit, without any art at all; he frequented the plays all his younger time, but in his elder days lived at Stratford, and supplied the stage with two plays every year, and for it had an allowance so large, that he spent at the rate of 1,000 pounds a year, as I have heard.'

"This strongly supports the theory that Shaxpur had got his hands on a load tof plays after TB was dead, or perhaps had been given them by TB in his lifetime, and was doling them out to the London theatres every year. Making a great deal of money out of it too."

Polly paused, and waited until a noisy piece of dialogue had been concluded on the rehearsal stage.

"Back to Jonson. He did something else to create a new reputation for Shaxpur, once he was safely dead. He went up to Stratford again and helped set up the tomb in the church. The statue in which he was originally depicted as a wool merchant was changed. There is a drawing of the original monument, which showed a man with a woolsack. This was altered to a quill and paper, probably at the time the inscriptions were written."

"So the Royal Court were paying Jonson to set up a cover story to bury the true identity of the Bard even more deeply, then?"

"Yes indeed. Jonson's pension was doubled by James I in the year after his accession. Whichever monarch was on the throne, Jonson got well looked after. And there was an outpouring of praise for him when he died in 1637, and he was buried in Westminster Abbey."

Polly was about to continue, but abruptly cut himself off when he saw Griselda looking over at them, script in hand. "Right, shall we press on? Polonius? Hamlet? Act II, scene 2. Everybody ready?"

Polly stepped on stage, drew an imaginary cloak about his shoulders, and raised his head to challenge the Sir.

"Do you know me , my Lord?"

"Excellent well. You are a fishmonger."

"Not I, my lord."

"Then I would you were so honest a man."

Hamish smiled. A fishmonger was a slang Elizabethan term for a brothel keeper. He slipped back out into the fresh air on the terrace, thinking hard about what he had learned. There was clearly more than met the eye in the life of the creator of *Hamlet*. Time he did some serious study on all this. If it wasn't Will Shaxpur, then who was the real writer? Four centuries after his death, the world still didn't know.

24

My tables! Meet it is I set it down
Act I, scene v

"Have you two finished your first course?" said the waitress, pushing a shock of titian red hair back from her face before reaching across them to take away their empty plates.

After working all morning, Hamish and Olivia felt they'd earned some lunch, and had found a table by the window in Carpaccio's. It was always busy at this time of day, being just across the road from the theatre.

"Everything all right for you?" This was said automatically. She was an attractive girl with a nice smile, whom Hamish had seen in the restaurant once or twice before.

"Yes, thanks, Annie," he said, smiling back at her. "A very tasty pizza. Lots of garlic and onions in it too. You *have* asked us twice already if it was all right for us, you know. And they'll ask me again at the till point, and I'll still say yes."

Annie grimaced.

"Okay, sorry, you know we have to do it? Hey, listen? I heard you talking about who Shakespeare was and all that stuff? You ought to talk to my grandad, he's got a bee in his bonnet about it. Says he's got something interesting about Shakespeare, a letter or something."

"Yeah? What does he say? I'd like to know."

118

"Dunno really, something about some diaries? Guy called Samuel something? Funny name? Peeps? Met someone who worked with Shakespeare? You'd have to ask Granddad. Coffees?"

"Yes please, two cappucinos." Hamish was amused as usual by the new speech mode that added a question mark to every statement. He fell into the rhythm. "I can get in touch with your granddad? What's his name?"

Annie was moving away from the table, her hands full.

"Harry, Harry King. 16 Elsinore Avenue – it's only ten minutes down the road," she called back over her shoulder, disappearing into the kitchens. "He'd be glad to have a chat, I know?"

"What do you think that's all about?" asked Olivia absently, flicking through her phone as she spoke.

"Sounds like Samuel Pepys," said Hamish. "Though what he's got to do with Willie Shaxpur, I've no idea. But wouldn't it be great if we could get some sort of proof of Oz's theory? So far it's all just hypothetical."

"Huh. You'll be lucky. Anyway, were Shakespeare and Pepys contemporaries? Surely not."

"Possibly, just about. Pepys was much younger, obviously. I did study him for a term, but I've forgotten most of it. Let's have a look at his dates, shall we?"

"Just a sec. I'll see." She tapped at her mobile.

A woman at the next table had a loud braying voice that carried across the room.

"I know although I'm her grandmother, heaven forbid I should interfere, but all I said was, don't they teach you how to use a knife and fork anymore? You should have heard the mouthful of abuse I got – not from her, from her mother! Honestly, darling, table manners today…"

"*Samuel Pepys, 1633 to 1703,*" Olivia read from her screen. "*Secretary to the Admiralty and famous diarist.*"

"Shakespeare – Polly's Shaxpur – died in 1616," mused Hamish. "Let's see now… so when Pepys was, say, in his twenties, there were still many older people in London who would have been alive in Shakespeare's day. Pepys could feasibly have talked to someone who remembered him. Wow."

"*Pepys wrote his diaries between 1660 and 1669,*" read Olivia. "So, yes, that's no problem."

"Right. Let's finish our coffees and go check this one out, baby. Don't know why, but I like the sound of it."

Olivia was pretending not to listen to the nearby conversation but was reluctant to follow him out and lose the end of it. If this person didn't have a huge Range Rover with two yellow Labradors in the back double parked outside, she'd be very surprised. The woman was peering at the menu. She had a grating voice to match her character.

"They've no artichokes, no guacamole… honestly, darling, it's like trying to eat out in East Berlin. Yes, I send Zarina these really super presents for her birthday and so on, and do you think I ever get a thank you letter? Never. Not once. Not even a text."

The woman's companion nodded, her jewellery jangling over the plate.

"I *know,* Celia! Tell me about it. You ought to do what I do. I send my nephew a cheque. He's only eleven, but of course he's got a bank account. Then I *forget* to sign it, don't I? That spurs the little b. into action all right. I get

120

indignant emails demanding I transfer the money online instead, as the bank has returned the cheque. Still no thank you, mind you, just an emoji of a long face."

Celia unconsciously made a similar face.

"Zarina wouldn't know what a cheque was if it sat up and bit her. And the names they give them these days. Zarina! I mean, for goodness' sake. Whatever happened to Carol and Sue, that's what I'd like to know? Let alone David and Mike, for that matter. Vanished into history, I suppose."

As Celia spoke she was digging into her plate of chicken Caesar salad. She viciously forked into an elusive tomato, which burst open with surprising force. The juice spurted across the gap between the two tables and onto Olivia's white T-shirt.

"Oh, shit!" Olivia cried instinctively, spilling her coffee onto its saucer. She stared down at the rapidly spreading red blob on her breast. Celia glanced disdainfully across at her for a moment, frowned in irritation at Olivia's expression, and carried on with her conversation as if nothing had happened. "And they're on their wretched mobiles all the time, even at mealtimes. This generation haven't the least consideration for other people. I keep telling them that manners simply means putting others before oneself, but do they listen…?"

Olivia was dabbing at the stain with a napkin that she'd dipped in the water jug, which only made matters worse. It was the second time she'd worn this particular top, which showed off her tan without being too revealing, and she liked it. She got to her feet. She pushed her coffee away unfinished.

"I'm just going to the loo to try and get this mark out," she said. "Then we'll go."

The chattering women didn't spare her a glance as she left. Hamish had been checking his phone as intently as any teenager. He looked across the room at the red-headed waitress and signalled for the bill. Annie smiled back at him and raised a hand in acknowledgement.

When she came over to the table with the bill, he noticed she had signed her name on the bottom.

"Annie H?" he said, peering at it as he pushed his credit card into the portable machine she was holding. "Not…"

The girl laughed.

"Yes, it's Hathaway, sorry. How stupid is that? You can imagine how I got teased at school? Have a great rest of the day and say hallo to my granddad."

And she moved away, leaving Hamish staring after her.

25

Sleeping within my orchard,
My custom always of the afternoon,
Upon my secure hour thy uncle stole,
With juice of cursed hebenon in a vial,
And in the porches of my ears did pour
The lep'rous distilment
Act 1, scene v

At a ten minutes' brisk walk from the restaurant they found Elsinore Avenue, a quiet road of respectable houses. Outside no. 16 an older man was standing on a stepladder, noisily trimming his privet hedge with an electric saw. He looked to be in his seventies, wiry, with a good head of white hair, who had caught the sun on his face and arms.

Hamish and Olivia stood watching for a moment, unwilling to interrupt. After a couple of minutes he noticed the couple standing expectantly, and clicked the motor off. He was wearing ear mufflers, which he pushed back off his head, wincing as he did so, and scratched his arm.

"Does my head in, this noise," he said, clambering down the ladder carefully to stand among the privet cuttings. "But it's a job that's got to be done. What can I do for you?"

"Mr King? Sorry to disturb you," said Hamish. "Er – we're from the theatre. We've just been talking to your granddaughter Annie in Carpaccio's. She thought you wouldn't mind if we had a chat with you. It's about who Shakespeare was. She mentioned Pepys' diaries?"

"Glad of a break, to be honest," said the old man, pressing his hand against his ear. "Yes, it's an intriguing story. Let's go inside. I'll see if my wife will make us a cup of tea. She…"

"No, really, we're fine," said Olivia. "Just had lunch."

But he had already opened the front door and was ushering them into the living room. It was very neat, plainly furnished, with no sign of any books, or pictures on the walls.

"We'd better take our shoes off, or there'll be hell to pay," he said. "Now, tell me what it's all about. Ah, Trudi my darling? We've got visitors."

A dark-haired woman had put her head round the door, clearly taken aback. She was in her early fifties, Olivia guessed, and very good looking in a sultry way. The two visitors introduced themselves and explained a little about why they were there. Trudi frowned at her husband, but after a short hesitation gestured to them to sit down.

"I'm just making a pot of tea. Perhaps you'll join us?"

"Er, well, actually we've only just…"

Olivia interrupted Hamish and said, "If you're sure that's no trouble, we'd love to."

Trudi pursed her lips and left the room. The old man looked uncomfortable.

"Sorry about that. We've got my brother Claude staying here with us from London for a few days, and Trudi's had a lot to do. He's a great deal better off than us, you see, and nothing seems…" He cleared his throat and stopped himself with an effort.

"Annie said something about a Samuel. I assume Samuel

Pepys, Mr King?" prompted Hamish, perching himself gingerly on a chintz-covered sofa, which reminded Olivia of her grandmother's house.

"Ah yes, it's quite a strange story. Very strange indeed really, if you're interested in that sort of thing. Let's see now…" He scratched his arm while he gathered his thoughts. Olivia noticed he was suffering from some kind of psoriasis, the arm looking raw and inflamed.

"You see, my grandmother was a schoolteacher. Lived in Stratford all her life, and had always been interested in Shakespeare, I suppose. She died when we were quite young. But I remember her showing us kids, me and my sister Lizzie, a cardboard box full of old letters, recipes and stuff from her family, and a hymnbook. The family had all lived in the same house for generations, you know. On the Clopton Road, it was. I don't really remember it, though." He sighed. "She had to leave it when she got older and went into a home. I think her money ran out. They've pulled it down years ago. It's all flats there now. Everything's flats these days, isn't it? The council…"

Hamish shifted uneasily and pushed his hair back. It was hot in the little room.

"Was there something about Shakespeare in it, Mr King?"

"Yes," said the old man with a flash of irritation. "I'm coming to that. There was a piece of paper in this box, something about Samuel Pepys meeting a man who had known Shakespeare. But my Nan said it was never in *The Diaries of Samuel Pepys*. It must have been edited out, she said. So this paper was important and we weren't to lose it after she'd gone."

Hamish flashed Olivia a glance.

"Can you remember what it said, Mr King?" he asked. "Sounds really interesting."

"I can do better than that," said the old man slowly. "I've still got the box upstairs somewhere with everything in it. Would you like me to try and find it for you? I'm pretty sure it's in the spare room."

As Hamish nodded, Trudi came in with a tray of tea things and some plain digestive biscuits. He quickly rose to help her put the tray down, and the woman gave the young man a tight-lipped smile. She had changed into a summer dress, showing off a suntan and long shapely legs.

"Help yourselves," she said. "I'll leave you to it. I'm just going to help Claude pack. He's leaving tomorrow."

The old man rose unsteadily to his feet.

"I'd had enough of that hedge cutting racket for the day, anyway. This ear's really painful. I'm glad you called and gave me an excuse to stop. I was so tired early on, I dropped off to sleep in the orchard. Didn't I, dear? That's when a wasp must have stung me."

He followed his wife out of the room. Olivia poured two cups of tea, and they each took a biscuit. After a moment, they both got their phones out. They sat in silence tapping away for a while before Mr King came down the stairs again.

He proudly handed them a piece of crinkled paper filled with spidery handwriting on both sides in faded brown ink, and sat down, puffing a little after his exertions.

"Told you I'd got it!" he said. "I had to move a few things to find it. Here you are. Nan thought it had been written by *her* grandmother."

Hamish and Olivia studied the document in silence, their heads close together. It was quite hard to decipher. After a while, Olivia sat back, shaking her head.

"Over to you, Ham," she said. "You're the Pepys scholar. What do you make of it?"

"Well," said Hamish, still peering the manuscript. "I'm no scholar at all really, but I think I've got most of it now that I've read it through a couple of times. It seems to be someone's version of an extract from Pepys' diaries. Maybe written from memory, and perhaps not very accurately. But I wouldn't really know."

"Well, read it out then! Don't keep us all in suspense."

"I'll try," said Hamish.

26

**Slanders, sir. For the satirical rogue says here
that old men have grey beards,
that their faces are wrinkled,
their eyes purging thick amber and plum-tree gum,
and that they have a plentiful lack of wit**
Act II, scene ii

"It reads something like this." Hamish started reading the notes out loud.

Samuel Pepys August 1662

Up and to the Lord Privy Seal's office, where I had much signing of papers and debate with Sir William until early evening. Then by ferry to the Mermaid Tavern. Purchased a lobster for sixpence from the [can't read this word, hang on] *wherryman, a surly villain, for the landlord to cook for my dinner if I were so disposed. Very merry company, and much talk and laughter, full of content on every side.*

Then took place an encounter worthy of remark. An old man of some eighty years sitting in the corner was said to have been an actor and worked with William Shakespeare himself. He was a big man, [I think it's] *rheumy and wet-eyed, glad enough to accept a tankard of mild ale from me for his story.*

His name was John Lowin, [looks like] *and he had indeed acted at The Rose Theatre and the Globe for many years. He said the man he knew as Will Shaxpur had been one of the company for a time. A very handsome fellow of great wit and beauty, he said, much admired by men and women alike.*

I asked him how Shakespeare had time to pen his most marvellous poesy and plays if working long hours in the theatre as an actor? The old man shook his head and said that to his mind Will Shaxpur was no writer at all, but a good enough actor. Yet his name was appended to the works of a truly great man, a noble lord who was besotted with his beauty.

'He loved to claim he was the author and waxed indignant when we scoffed! An upstart crow, we called him! And rightly so. And yet did he often brag that his name would go down in history!' His laughter was as the cackling of a cockerel among a crowd of chickens.

What did become of him? I inquired. The old man scratched his hairless head, and then told me Will had retired to the country quite young and was rumoured to have purchased a large house by the Avon. How he had come by the means to do such was a mystery to all.

'They do say he had a loose tongue, i'faith, which did cause him an untimely end. Poisoned and drownded, poor soul,' he said.

I was moved to inquire further, but at this juncture my dinner was served by the maid. She was a comely red-headed young wench with fine bosoms. I did fumble under her skirt as she bent over my table but was repulsed, although she later hath given me kisses when I took my leave and allowed me some access to her person.

Sadly I was then too much in my cups to make full advantage. I called for a ferry, being weary, and the hour being late. And so to bed.

27

Hamlet: "Do you see yonder cloud that's almost in shape of a camel?
Polonius: By the mass, and 'tis like a camel, indeed.
Hamlet: Methinks it is like a weasel.
Polonius: It is backed like a weasel.
Hamlet: Or like a whale?
Polonius: Very like a whale."
Act III, scene ii

Hamish looked up.

"Randy old bugger, Pepys, wasn't he?" he said.

"We'll call that male chauvinist sexual harassment then, late medieval style, shall we?" said Olivia, for the sake of something to say. Hamish started perusing the writing again. There was a long silence, which Mr King broke.

"What do you think?" he asked, reaching out to retrieve the document.

"I honestly don't know," said Hamish, reluctant to release it. "Er – would you mind if I hung on to this for a bit? Show it to someone who knows what they're talking about? I'd take very good care of it."

The old man looked alarmed.

"Oh, no, sorry. I'm afraid I couldn't possibly let you do that. It's been in my family for generations, you see. Besides…" He hesitated. "It might be valuable, mightn't it?

I mean, you never know these days. Some of these antiques programmes on the telly… You see, Trudi is very fond of nice clothes, and I…."

"No, of course we understand," Olivia intervened hastily. "Not a problem. I tell you what though – would you have any objection to me taking a photograph of it?" She held up her phone. "So that we can study it a bit more later?"

"Wonderful gadget, that, isn't it?" said Mr King. "My son's got one. He can even ask it questions, and it answers him back! No, go ahead. I don't mean to be obstructive. It's just that…"

"We quite understand," said Hamish. "Can you get a good image of it, Ol?"

Olivia was already clicking away.

"Yes, no probs. I'll take three or four. Thanks very much, Mr King." She handed the precious document back to him, and they rose to go.

He showed them to the door. The blue sky had become overcast, and big raindrops were beginning to spatter the pavements.

"Well, goodbye, and nice to meet you," said Mr King. "I hope it was of some interest to you. Oh oh, looks as if you're going to get wet." He was pressing his hand against his ear again.

"Don't worry. You go inside, sir," said Hamish, taking Olivia's arm. "We'll run for it – we haven't far to go. Thanks again, Mr King and say thank you to Mrs King for us. Your late great-great-grandmother did a good job."

"Funny thing, now I come to recall it," said Mr King, retreating into the doorway. He chuckled. "Hathaway is a name that runs through my family. Makes you think, doesn't it?"

They broke into a jog, waving goodbye as they went.

"God, this is dynamite, isn't it? Oz is going to be pretty chuffed. This is exactly the sort of thing he's been hoping for," said Hamish. The rain was falling harder now, splashing back up from the pavement. The gutters were already starting to gurgle, and a long grumble of thunder sounded in the distance.

"I don't know about that, but I do know that I'm getting soaked to the skin," said Olivia, hunching her shoulders as they ran. "My new trainers are going to be ruined. I don't think the Bard will like this, Ham. Honestly, I don't."

She shivered a little, ducking her head.

"Look at that cloud," said Hamish. "Don't you think it looks like a camel?"

"Yes, but no doubt it's backed like a whale. Come on, you fool. Let's not hang about, let's just get home."

The rain pelted down harder than ever as the sky turned a menacing inky black. The thunder rolled above them like the growling of an angry giant, and the first forks of summer lightning stabbed the sky.

28

Bernardo: 'Tis here!
Horatio: 'Tis here!
Marcellus: 'Tis gone!
Act I, scene i

Back in the flat they changed out of their damp clothes. Olivia came out of the bedroom in a velvet sleepsuit, running a brush through her hair. She settled herself on the sofa, flicking on the television menu, then turned the set off again with a sigh.

"Hang on," said Hamish, emerging from the kitchen with two mugs of green tea. "Just had a new delivery from Attic Tea. Try this. Chinese Jasmine Pearl, very relaxing. And before you start goggling at the telly, I want to have another look at that manuscript and text it to Oz."

Olivia fished her phone out of her bag and found the photographs.

"No writer at all?" said Hamish. "This is sensational, you know. Someone who actually met Shaxpur. I'm going to call Oz."

There was silence until the phone was answered.

"Hi Oz, it's Ham. You ok? Listen, here's something incredible. You'll never guess what we've got for you. This is going to blow the literary world sky high. No, I'm not kidding." He told Oz something of their afternoon visit to Mr King, and what he had shown them. Olivia could hear from the squawks that Oz was excited. Hamish answered a few questions, then rang off and turned to her.

"What did he say?"

"He said, and I quote, 'totes amazeballs'. I'm to send the pics to him on WhatsApp now."

They glanced through them, their heads together, Hamish's arm around Olivia. They read the words again.

"'*He was no writer at all, but a good enough actor*'? Jeez! Can you imagine what they will make of that? Bragged '*that his name would go down in history*'. What does this mean? Oz is going to love this. Just sending them… *Shit!* Where have they gone?" Hamish peered anxiously at the little screen.

"Give it here," said Olivia. "I know my own phone better than you do. They must be… Ham, have you deleted them by mistake?"

"I haven't done a thing except press 'Send'," protested Hamish. "They must be there somewhere. We've got to print them off at this end as well."

"You'll be lucky," said Olivia. "It's weird, but they really have disappeared."

She frowned. The mobile burst into its merry little tune, and she put it to her ear.

"Oh, hi, Oz. Did you get the pics? Ham has only gone and lost them, would you believe. Oh, you did, thank goodness. What do you reckon? Here, you have a word with him."

Hamish put his mug of steaming tea down carefully and took the phone.

"Yes, mind blowing. Yes, I agree. The most important real

glimpse of Shaxpur's actual life ever. And that entry never appeared in Pepys' published diaries. Going to print them out? You're right, good idea. Yes, I'll hold on."

Hamish turned to Olivia, pressing the mobile to his chest. "He's over the moon. Going to sell this story to the world. Says it's worth millions."

"*What?* He better hadn't. My God. We'll never work in Stratford again!" Olivia's shoulders went up, and she looked shaken. "Can't you just imagine the reaction. It doesn't bear thinking about, Ham!"

Hamish waved her away with a smile.

"He's only kidding, silly. Hello? Hello, Oz? Have you printed them off?" He suddenly looked serious and sat up straight. "You what? You've lost them as well? What the bloody hell is going on?"

After a further brief conversation, he clicked the phone off and turned to Olivia, an expression of astonishment on his face.

"He got the photos and he read the piece twice. Then when he tried to print them, they just disappeared. Same as on your phone."

They sat in silence for a moment, trying to take it all in.

"The most sensational literary discovery of the century, and it's totally vanished," said Hamish, shaking his head in disbelief. "Now there's only our word for it. And who's going to believe us, three silly young actors with an axe to grind? Nobody at all."

"No, nobody at all," said Olivia. "The story's a non-starter." She suddenly clapped her hands together and let out a cry of joy. "*Yeess!!* What a relief! You know something? The

Bard can sleep easy in his grave again, the crafty old bugger. What could be a better result than that? Put that tea away and let's open a bottle of Prosecco to celebrate!"

"Okay, I'll put some music on – a bit of Adele I think. And after that I'll have some of that Shiraz you've been hiding." Hamish stood up and walked over to the window. "Let's get that bloody wine open. I feel like getting rat-arsed."

"Aren't you forgetting something?" said Olivia, coming back from the kitchen with two long stemmed glasses and a bottle of Prosecco. She handed it over to Hamish to pop the cork. "I'm surprised you haven't suggested that we go back to Mr King and have another go at photographing that piece of paper?"

Hamish groaned.

"Nah, I'm not going all the way over there again now. It's still pouring with rain. I'll call in the morning. Nothing's going to happen to it overnight."

"Well, don't say you haven't been warned. I didn't take to that foxy wife of his. Mm, this is nice. Cheers."

Adele's distinctive music was playing in the background. Olivia touched her glass to Hamish's, and they drank together.

"I know, let's rehearse one of our scenes. You've got to keep in training for when your big day comes, you know."

"Ha bloody ha. As if."

But after a moment he put his glass down and lifted her chin gently with his hand.

"Soft you now, the fair Ophelia. Nymph, in thy orisons be all my sins remembered!"

Olivia looked up at him, and his heart jumped at her closeness.

Two hours later they were still debating nuances of delivery. The remains of Welsh rarebit were on the little table, along with several empty glasses, coffee cups and an ashtray.

"That's the wine gone, and now you're on the Scotch," said Olivia. "I've had enough. That was a useful session, but I'm shattered. I'm off to bed. Don't stay up too late."

"I'm fine," said Hamish indistinctly, pouring himself another measure. "Just going to have this, and maybe another joint, and ponder the deeds of the day. I keep thinking about what Polly said about Ben Jonson, I don't know why. If he was involved with publishing the Folios, he stood to make a lot of money. He wouldn't want Will Shaxpur blabbering and wanting a share of it, would he? I tell you one thing, Ol. I'm going to solve this mystery if it's the last thing I do."

Olivia looked hard at him and opened her mouth to say something but decided against it. She kissed him full on the lips and went into the bedroom.

It was over an hour before Hamish joined her, stumbling against a chair as he undressed. Olivia didn't stir as he came out of the bathroom and got into bed with her. He was soon in a deep sleep. It wasn't long before he was dreaming.

Dreaming, dreaming....

29

**Oh God, I could be bounded in a nutshell,
and count myself a king of infinite space,
were it not that I have bad dreams**
Act II, scene ii

The Falcon Inn, Bidford-on Avon. 22 April 1616.

I'm in a pub. It's crowded, noisy, merry, but it isn't like any other pub I know. For one thing the clothes of the occupants are not T-shirts, jeans and trainers, but the garments of an earlier age.

I must be in a play. That's it. I'm on stage. But the place is filthy. And it stinks. There are chamber pots in one corner, some of them overflowing. The straw covering the stone floor is matted with food and liquids. Skinny dogs are sniffing around, cocking their legs against the wooden benches and tables. In another corner, a boy is strumming on a mandolin and singing quietly, though no words can be discerned over the hubbub. And I'm not really Ham. I'm leaner, darker, older, different somehow. Hard to explain. But different.

I know the man standing beside me, who shoves a dog away with a kick to the ribs, cursing the animal and smoothing down his velvet doublet fastidiously. Ben Jonson is a big man in his forties, well dressed, with curly black hair falling over a white neck ruff. His brown eyes and fleshy nose jut out above a full mouth.

By his side is a smaller man, older and thinner, with a receding hairline and a grey beard. Michael Drayton has a scholarly air about him, and is quieter than Jonson, who smiles at me.

"Good to see you again, Will! You're looking better than ever."

They've come all the way from London especially to see me, I think. I'm flattered, but puzzled, and uneasy. Something isn't right. What am I reminded of?

"My excellent good friends! How dost thou?"

"Well enough," says Jonson, grinning back. "But how are you, Will? In hearty spirits, I trust?"

"In perfect health and memory, God be praised."

"You have lost none of your good looks. But it is some time since you were in London town, acting in our Globe. They were good days."

"Indeed. And I was in one of your own plays, Master Jonson."

"Yes, but more often in the works of a far greater genius than me. Now sadly gone from us, but his legacy is mankind's forever, thank the Lord."

It hurts me to think of him dead.

"Was his death much spoken of in London?"

"Very little. No tributes were paid. But those of us who know the truth will be ever in mourning. For truly, I did love the man, this side idolatry." Jonson sighs and shakes his head. "Thank the Lord, he left many more of his immortal plays, though as you well know, several needed completing by other hands, the so-called collaborators. Long after his death, of course." He chuckles and says to Drayton, "Can you imagine for one moment the Bard collaborating with another writer during his lifetime?"

We all laugh. The three of us are drinking ale out of large mustard coloured tankards. None of us is smoking, though the air is thick with clouds of tobacco from a dozen clay pipes around the room, and my eyes are stinging. Two women are ladling a lumpy grey mess into chipped bowls for those customers who have pennies to spare to buy potage. The younger of the women looks across and smiles at me, brushing the hair out of her eyes. All around us is chatter and laughter, punctuated by the odd shout from the card table. Images flicker, draw near and then recede. Weirdly, somewhere in the distance, I can hear a car horn sounding and the hum of motor traffic outside my bedroom window.

"You've done well for yourself, Will," says Jonson above the din, waving his tankard around in indication of my success. "You've got a good name as a businessman in Stratford now, I hear. You invested your windfall well enough."

"Aye, true enough, Master Jonson. Property will never fail you. And the town's growing these days. It's good to have something put by."

"And what of Anne, and your children?" Jonson asks slyly, but I merely shrug. "Things move on. She has long found someone else."

"You've made a will, as I suggested in my letter?"

I look sharply at him.

"I have, as it happens, though what concern it is of yours I know not. I am in the best of health, sir. Oh, and I even remembered to leave something to Anne, which is more than she deserves." I laugh and swig some more beer.

"And you've got more than land, haven't you, Will? You have a very nice collection of manuscripts, have you not?" says the other with a smile, cocking his head on one side. Michael Drayton has a house not far from Stratford, and another in London. He looks more like a lawyer than a writer. But he is a well-respected poet of considerable prominence. And a shrewd enough man of the world.

"What mean you, sir?" I reply, knowing the answer very well. "More than land?"

"Those play scrips have been a very good source of income for you, meting them out to the theatres year by year, have they not? But I fear your supply is now exhausted."

I am about to deny this, seeking words to express my indignation, when I am saved the trouble.

"We have them all now, I am nearly sure, and it is time to print them all for the world to benefit," says Jonson. "But there is one more service you can do for posterity. Did you bring the manuscript of *Hamlet*, as also requested in the message that I sent?"

The two men are looking keenly at me now, and their manner has become more intense.

"Indeed, I have it here, sirs," I say, tapping the well-worn leather bag on my shoulder, and looking down fondly at it. "One of my dearest possessions, and full of good memories. But may I enquire why you gentlemen are so eager to see it?"

"The King's Players are performing *Hamlet* again next year for His Majesty, and I have some small interest in the enterprise," says Jonson. He looks around him at his surroundings and lifts the tankard to his lips. "All the plays need editing and then publishing, and I have found the men to do it. *Aah* - I do so delight me of this country ale. London beer is but thin and dirty stuff."

He quaffs his ale, then slowly sets his tankard down on the table.

"Yes, the two quartos of *Hamlet* differ not a little, and I have the notion that yours may throw light on several ambiguities. After all, the copy you have is the original used for the first production of the play, is't not? Did you yourself not play a part in it?"

"I did indeed, sir!" I say proudly. "I played the ghost of Hamlet's father and was accounted a good actor."

"I am certain of it, sir. May we see what you have?" says Jonson. An old man in rough country garb stumbles into him and he swiftly tugs his tankard to his chest. "Have a care, man!" The yokel totters off snarling about haughty London folk, then trips over a dog looking up at him with pleading eyes.

By good chance the party of card players at the nearby table have finished their game and are now taking noisy farewells of each other. We move into their chairs round the narrow table and sit down. I reluctantly produce the sheaf of yellowing papers from my bag, and lay them out, carefully wiping away the smears of spilt ale with my sleeve.

The bulky figure of the landlord looms over us.

"Master Copeland!" I cry. "Just in time, sirrah!"

The landlord wipes his large hands on the dirty apron round his waist and collects up the empty tankards of the card players.

"Halloa, gentlemen. Do not tell me Master Will is still boasting of the plays he wrote in London town?" He grins and squints down at the top page of the bundle. "*The Tragical History of Hamlet, Prince of Denmark*, By William Shake-speare. Ha! But now we hear it wasn't you who wrote them at all? Now there's a surprise." His stomach wobbles with laughter. "He's a lovely lad, is our Will. Oh dear me, yes. A nicer fellow I never met, bless ye. But can you imagine him with a quill in his hand? More ale then, gentlemen? Yes indeed."

He goes off to the kitchen with his hands full, still shaking his head and laughing. I feel my face flushing with embarrassment.

"I did write!" I protest. "I wrote a play – well, part of a play. And some classical verses too. I was..." But Jonson cuts me off.

"Yes, Will. I read them. Small Latin and less Greek, indeed. Never mind. We know the truth, but few do, and fewer still with every passing year. And you were very well rewarded for the use of your name, just as long as you kept your mouth shut, weren't you?" His tone suddenly changes. "Do you remember solemnly swearing never to reveal the secret, not even by implication?"

Swear, says the old Mole. A voice in my head is declaiming. *Swear!*

And suddenly and unaccountably I feel cold.

30

What wilt thou do? Thou wilt not murder me?
Act III, scene iv

"Remember? But you did talk about it, didn't you, Will? You've been blabbering about your big payday. So loudly that we have heard you in London. And we can't have that, can we?"

So that's what they are doing here. *'Were you not sent for? My lord, we were sent for.'* It is clear to me now that they are playing Rosencrantz and Guildenstern to my Hamlet.

"No, no, I never...," I stammer. I feel the blood pumping in my head. But Jonson cuts me off with a gesture, and I am silent.

"Drink deep, sir. This is fine ale indeed."

We all raise fresh tankards while Jonson thumbs through the screed of paper, holding the sheets short-sightedly to his face.

"Ah yes, that's better... this makes more sense. See'st thou this scene, Drayton? This is just what we want. Ah, and that other scene has gone altogether, I see..."

They put their heads together, excluding me. I feel an urgent need to empty my bladder. I stand up. This door? Or this? There must be somewhere to go to pee. Is that a police siren in the distance? Or a television set on somewhere?

Out of the corner of my eye, I see Jonson pulling a phial from his pouch and pouring some white powder into the tankard I have left on the table. Drayton has moved between us to block my line of sight. Jonson thinks I haven't seen what he is doing. My London friends... *'Whom I will trust as I would adders fanged'*...

I stare at him. What? Why has he done that? That can't be right. I mustn't drink it. Yet somehow now I am drinking it, and my head is spinning and the conversation has got louder and the inn is noisier than ever and a mobile phone is beeping urgently.

"You've had a tad too much," says a voice softly in my ear. "Best to sleep it off, Master Will. We'll look after you. Even make you a fine tomb. Yes, a very fine monument, so that your name will live forever. Well, it is your name on the plays, isn't it?"

Somebody laughs. I sip some more ale, but now my legs feel weak, as if they don't belong to me. What is this thundering noise in my head?

"I shall undertake the wording on the tomb myself. Good night, sweet Swan of Avon. Let's see how well you can swim, shall we?"

Now a strong arm is around my shoulder and I am outside in the air and I can see the starry firmament and breathe the strong river smell. An owl hoots from a treetop, a long low melancholy sound.

It's cold here under the arch of the ancient bridge, and I try to pull my cloak over to protect myself. The sound of the river is louder now and I desperately need to pee. Something or someone is pushing me down to the dark waters. My innards are churning, my heart hammering fit to burst. There's a terrible pain in my stomach. '*No, no, the drink, the drink, the drink! O my dear Hamlet! The drink, the drink! I am poisoned.*'

I try to speak, but no words will come. It's too late. And the water is so cold...

"*Ham! Ham! It's all right.* Wake up!"

"What? What?"

"You're having a nightmare. You've pulled the duvet off us! It's really cold."

"*Urrgh.* Oh, my head. Sorry, sorry."

Hamish pulled himself up and sat with his head in his hands.

"Yes, bad dream. I was under a bridge... I'd been poisoned. But somehow it wasn't me. I think I was drowning too. God, must have a pee."

He padded off to the bathroom. Olivia tried to rearrange the bedclothes in the dark.

"Drink some water!" she called sleepily. "You got really pissed last night, you know. And hurry up – I want to go back to sleep. It's after three in the morning." She turned on her side. There was no traffic now.

Hamish returned to bed and lay back on the pillows, his arm around her bare back. He was trembling.

"I was having the most amazing dream," he said. "I was in some pub with Ben Jonson and Michael Drayton. I think I was Willie Shaxpur… they were trying to murder me. Yes, they poisoned me. Then I was drowning. No, it's fading already. Something about a bundle of papers, important."

"It's just a dream, Ham. Too much wine. And whisky too!"

"They murdered Shaxpur to keep the Bard's identity secret, and they wanted to make money out of the publication of the Folio. Will had somehow acquired a lot of the original manuscripts of the plays, which he'd sold covertly over the years. But now they were common property, and he'd run out of any new ones, so his usefulness was over. He knew too much, and had to go. Then they could set up the legend of him as the writer, which they couldn't do while he was alive. So they… Ol?"

Hamish looked down at her fair head, but she had fallen back to sleep. He sighed and settled down beside her, his head nestling in the nape of her neck, his arms round her. He felt as if he'd had an insight into a horrible fate. Was it a warning? He could still smell the river water, dank and musty, as strange images chased through his mind. But soon they disappeared with him into the dark.

31

The story is extant, and writ in very choice Italian
Act III, scene ii

"Do you want me to make us some breakfast? I don't have to go into the theatre till a bit later this morning. How's your head?"

The sun was streaming through the window into the little living room, and Radio One was chattering about school runs and birthdays between its bursts of thumping music and repetitive lyrics.

Hamish came out of the bathroom in a towelling gown over his Calvin Klein boxer shorts. He had showered and cleaned his teeth, and felt a lot better for it. Olivia was standing at the kitchen door, frying pan in hand. She was wearing just a T-shirt, and the fair down on her bare legs and arms showed up in the sunlight.

"Better, thanks. Never thought I'd say this, but I actually fancy a fry up. Meant to be a good hangover cure."

"And some black coffee. Have you got over your nightmare?"

Hamish sat at the table and pulled some books towards him.

"Yes, thanks. Very odd, that. Most realistic. Listen, changing the subject, do you want to hear about my exciting research? If our local hero didn't write the plays, then who did? Would you like to hear about my candidate?"

Olivia was now busy cooking at the worktop and called out over the kitchen clatter that she'd rather wait until they were sitting down. Ten minutes later she brought out two plates of fried eggs, bacon, mushrooms, and onions, and a rack of toast. Hamish poured out the coffee, and they tucked in with relish. She ate much more slowly than him, chewing every mouthful. But Olivia finally pushed her empty plate away.

"Okay. Let's have it then," she said.

"Right. Someone in London who was incredibly well educated actually wrote the plays. How would you like a guy who was brought up in Queen Elizabeth's court, went to both Oxford and Cambridge to study philosophy and classics, and read law as well? He ran groups of actors and was known as a leading writer and poet in his youth. He was such a brilliant scholar that his tutor gave up on him when he was fourteen, saying he had nothing more to teach him."

"Wow. I'm impressed. What else?" Olivia buttered some toast and munched it slowly. "Pour me some more coffee?"

"Of course." Hamish topped up both cups. "You know that thirteen of the plays are set in Italy?"

"Yes, you said so, darling."

"Well, this man travelled to Italy for a year when he was in his twenties and was mad about the place. He went to Venice, Florence, Verona, Pisa, and Sicily. All mentioned in the plays, incidentally, and even in their titles. He also loved Italian fashion, so much so that when he came back to court in England, he was known as 'the Italian'. He is even said to have brought an attractive young Italian back with him, a tenor. Imagine that."

"That must have caused a bit of a stir back at the Court. I wonder what his wife made of it! What sort of man was he?"

"Extravagant. Went through his inheritance pretty quickly. Witty, likeable, immensely erudite. Married twice, as well as having affairs with both women and young men. Given to bouts of melancholy."

"Sounds as though he kept himself busy one way or another," said Olivia.

Hamish nodded.

"Awesome to think we might be describing the real Shakespeare here. The actual one, I mean, not the pretty boy from Stratford with the similar name. Man of letters, traveller, and lover. The real McCoy. Impressed so far?"

"Obviously, though I don't think I'd want to be married to him. But I sense a snag coming?"

"Yeah, well, kind of. He died in 1604, and yet the plays kept on coming for another nine years afterwards. Oops."

"Well, that's the end of him then. Good. You know my views. The man from Stratford wrote the plays and the sonnets, and nothing's going to persuade me otherwise."

"Yeah, yeah, yeah."

Olivia looked at her watch and got up. She dabbed some grease off her chin with a tissue.

"I'd better not hang around. I'm due at the theatre soon. Will you clear up?"

"Sure. Just making a few more notes. Then I'm going to go back to Mr King's house to try and get hold of that Pepys document again. It is an incredibly important fragment of literary history. He has to be made to understand that.

And at this moment we've got absolutely no documentary proof it even exists."

He paused and wrinkled his nose.

"I wonder why that particular entry didn't get into the published diaries? It's really creepy, the way no references to the Bard can be found anywhere. There's been a very determined movement to preserve his anonymity from the very first, and it's not even over yet."

Hamish shook his head. He pushed the breakfast things away and started reading through one of the books, occasionally tapping at his laptop. When Olivia came out of the bedroom twenty minutes later, dressed and ready for the day, he didn't look up.

She kissed the top of his head and let herself out into another bright, sunny day. Already the streets were full of visitors, intent on visiting the Birthplace and the archives, and all the other landmarks commemorating Stratford's famous son. She smiled at the thought of Hamish's researches, and walked briskly down to the river, on to the theatre. It would take more than some scraps of gossip about some privileged Tudor aristocrat to change her mind about William Shakespeare, Gent, being the writer. Or even an excerpt from an alleged missing page of Pepys's diaries.

Mind you, she had to admit a feeling of unease after hearing so much debate from the others. Was there a doubt forming, somewhere deep in her subconscious? She shook her head to clear it of any such thoughts. It could lead to dangerous, muddy waters…

32

O villain, villain, smiling, damnèd villain!
My tables! Meet it is I set it down
That one may smile, and smile, and be a villain
Act 1, scene v

Hamish too was glad to be out in the fresh air an hour or two later. He stepped out briskly towards the avenue where Mr King lived, as he thought about the importance of the alleged entry in Pepys' diary.

True, it was only a handwritten version of a part of the diary that had for some reason been edited out of the official editions. But its revelation about Shakespeare - Shaxpur - not being a writer was incendiary stuff. It ought at least to lead to a close examination by experts about its possible authenticity, and raise a new clamour about the authorship debate. A lawyer might term it 'hearsay' evidence, but it was nonetheless a very valuable document.

In the garden the hedge cuttings were still lying untidily on the grass where they had fallen. Hamish frowned as he rang the doorbell. He could hear voices in the house, so felt it polite to wait before pressing the buzzer again.

This time the door was opened by a dark middle-aged man with a neatly cut beard. He wore an expensive looking sweater and immaculate black Gucci loafers. Hamish guessed he must be Mr King's brother, Claude. He had that subtle air of superiority that visitors from London to the provinces manage to exude. Their clothes, their haircuts, the very way they hold themselves, speak somehow of a different world, thought Hamish.

"Yes?" he said, the smile plastered across his face in sharp contrast with the coldness in his eyes. "We're rather busy at the moment, I'm afraid."

"Er, I'm from the theatre. I was here yesterday with my friend? We were talking to Mr King. Could I speak to him, please?"

"I'm afraid that isn't possible. May I ask what your interest is?"

Hamish hesitated and was about to reply, when the figure of Trudi appeared in the hallway coming down the staircase behind Claude.

"Oh, Mrs King," said Hamish. "I'm sorry to bother you again, but..."

"I'm afraid you've come at a bad time," she gulped. Her long dark hair was now swept loosely down her back, and it was clear she had been crying. She was wearing a lot more makeup than on the previous day, contrasting with her pallor and strained expression. "After you left, my husband said he didn't feel at all well and went up to bed. In the middle of the night his ear became so painful that we had to take him to hospital. I've never seen him so ill." Her voice broke. "It was terrible. We were in A&E for hours. They were very good, but...."

Claude put his arm round her protectively, and she leant her head on his shoulder. He stroked her bare neck soothingly, and she moved even closer to him. "We've only just got back," he said. "He died in the hospital. An acute reaction to the wasp sting, they said."

Hamish stepped back, staggered at the news. He knew Mr King had been in severe pain the previous day, but his death was totally unexpected. He expressed the conventional sentiments. The couple made no move to invite him in from the doorstep. He turned to leave, then plucked up his courage.

"Um, I know this is totally the wrong time," he stammered, "but you remember that document he showed me yesterday? Do you think I could possibly have another look at it? You see, it's very important."

"It certainly is," said Claude, the smile on his face slowly becoming a sneer. "An extract from Pepys' diary saying that Shakespeare wasn't really much of a writer? Fetch a few bob when the time's right, I should say, wouldn't you?"

"If I could just…"

"Not on your life, sunshine."

The smile had disappeared completely now, leaving deep tracks on his face.

"That's staying under lock and key. My brother may not have known its value, but I can assure you that we do. Don't we, darling?"

His arm still round Trudi's slim shoulders, he kissed her on the cheek. She looked down at the floor.

"Now if you'll excuse us, you'll understand we've got a lot to do. We'll have to come and see your little play some time, won't we, mouse? Goodbye!"

With the door slammed firmly in his face, Hamish was

left standing on the step with his mouth open. He raised his hand to knock on the door again, then thought better of it. He walked slowly home, stunned. All he could think of was the stricken look on Trudi's face. And the smile on Claude's.

33

The beauty of thy budding name
Sonnet 9

"Well, you know that's just amazing," said Olivia as they lay back on the bed together the next morning. "Quite incredible."

"Why, thank you, madam. Our aim is to give complete satisfaction at all times." Hamish sat up on one elbow and pushed the hair out of his eyes.

"I'm not talking about your efforts in bed, you fool," giggled Olivia, getting up naked and peering at her face for a moment in the dressing table mirror. She went briefly into the bathroom and came back to select something to wear. "I'm talking about your man, 'the Italian'. I've been trying to get him out of my head, but I have to admit it isn't easy. Anyway, you still haven't told me who he was."

"No, and there's a whole lot more. It's pretty obvious that the Bard put an awful lot of himself into *Hamlet*. There are a lot of so-called coincidences. He was a young man when he wrote it too."

He loved watching Olivia dress. She was so graceful even doing something as mundane as pulling on her tights. I'm falling, he thought. Falling, falling…

She stood up, straightening her dress.

"Incidentally, it looks as if you can write off any idea about

156

using Mr Pepys to bolster your theories. Those photos of the document are lost, and I can't really remember what the thing said even if you can. There's no way you're going to get poor Mr King's nasty brother to part with it, that's for sure."

"I know," said Hamish miserably. "It's a real pain. That bastard Claude. Grinning all over his face, while... Oz is badly hacked off about it."

"Seems like the whole thing's a complete cock-up," said Olivia. "Never mind, you tried."

"Seems, madam? I know not seems. Nay, is."

"Very good, Lord Hamlet. Anyway, getting back to your Bard, who *was* he then?" She came up to Hamish and gripped his shoulders, looking deep into his eyes. "Does he have a name?"

Hamish wriggled out of her grasp.

"Ow! Your nails are digging in." He heaved himself up and sat on the side of the bed. "Yes, he does. His name was Edward de Vere, and he was the 17th Earl of Oxford."

"Was he now?" said Olivia, impressed in spite of herself. "Tell me more."

"Well, his father, the 16th Earl, was immensely rich, and well in with the court. He gave Edward the best education possible. His tutor had one of the most extensive libraries in the land."

"Is that the one who said he had no more to teach him?"

"It is indeed. A precocious young genius. His father left him a handful of superb properties and estates when he died. But our Edward hadn't a clue about money. He sold everything off bit by bit to pay his debts, and ended up having to be subsidised by the Queen."

"Too busy writing poems and plays and having affairs all over the place, apparently," said Olivia.

"No doubt. As I told you, he was also married twice and had three daughters and one son, Henry, who became the 18th Earl of Oxford. Henry died aged18."

"That's sad. What did Edward look like? Are there any descriptions of him?"

"Yes, several. One said he was 'only a little fellow'. He was lame, but very attractive to both women and men, as I said before, and a leader of fashion. He was also known as witty and 'with a penetrating judgement'. Unlike poor Shaxpur, there is plenty of documentary evidence about him."

"Sounds like Byron. Tell me more."

"He was known to be highly intelligent and a man of letters. He was born in 1550 and was reported to have died in his hall at Hackney in 1604 on June 24th. But there is no record of his funeral, and he was simply never mentioned after that day, although he was the premier Earl of England. It's as if he disappeared off the face of the earth." Hamish groaned. "There's another very strange thing. On that day, King James sent officials very hurriedly to Hackney and it is said that they destroyed a lot of de Vere's possessions and papers. It's horrible to think what priceless manuscripts were lost."

"So you say that's why we have no literary fragments of Shakespeare's work?"

"Yep. Not a scrap survives. There is some evidence though that not everything was lost, but was taken to Windsor Castle of all places. Incidentally there was a fire there a hundred years later, and everything was burned. Wouldn't you just know it."

"Why Windsor, I wonder?" asked Olivia. Hamish knew that it was her home town, where her father was a local GP. "Well, the castle was one of Elizabeth's favourite royal residences. She was mad on theatre and even formed her own group of players, The Queen's Men. My guess is that de Vere spent a lot of time there, writing and producing plays, and would have known the town well. It seems he spent some of his childhood there too, and a period, convalescing from illness, in his twenties. There happens to be a play called *The Merry Wives of Windsor*, as you very well know. And the name Windsor occurs so many times in his works. Poor old Stratford never once, incidentally, but that needn't surprise anybody. The writer had probably never even been there."

Olivia let out a screech.

"Oh, there you go again. And I was just beginning to get interested. But I love the Windsor connection. My father thinks that some of the local Berkshire dialect phrases appear in the plays, did you know that?"

"Never heard that, but certainly the characters in the play have sometimes been identified with real people from the town."

"You ought to talk to my dad about it. But I'm not getting involved." Olivia paused. "Admittedly there is something about Mr de Vere that I like the sound of, I don't know why. He seems a bit special somehow, I'll give you that."

"Lord Oxford, if you don't mind, who also happened to be Lord Great Chamberlain of England. Don't tell me you're a convert now?"

"No way. I don't actually believe a word of it. You're welcome to tell Polly and Oz all about it, but I have no intention of offending Shakespeare's Shadow, thank you very much." She put her face very close to his, and pinched his stomach between her finger and thumb. "I've got to go. You're getting a bit flabby, you know. Too many pints of Hooky and not enough exercise. Time you hit the gym, *mon ami*."

"Hey!" Hamish protested, sitting up and pushing her hand away. "*O that this too, too solid flesh would melt*, eh? I get plenty of exercise living with you, thank you! But I will go down to the gym. Good idea. Where's my tracksuit?"

"On the floor of the wardrobe where you left it last time. Or would be if I hadn't picked it up for you. I don't know why I bother."

Hamish gave her a sweet smile and pecked her on the cheek as she left.

34

The theatre gym wasn't crowded, and many of the actors were busy elsewhere. The first thing Hamish saw was the athletic figure of Oz, heaving on the rowing machine. Hamish took the vacant machine beside him and slapped him on the back as a greeting. They fell easily into a rhythm together.

"Any more on de Vere?" said Oz, puffing only slightly.

"Well, apart from the minor inconvenience of his death in 1604, everything fits amazingly well with him being TB. The Bard. It's screaming out to those that have eyes to see."

"TB or not TB, eh? That is the question."

"Ha ha. Very funny. Tell you what you'll like though, Oz. He left some clues in the sonnets. In fact some people say that when the words 'very' or 'every' comes up, you can often find a cryptic allusion to his own real name. The big one is in 'Sonnet 76' which has the otherwise inexplicable line *that <u>every word </u>doth almost tell my name*. It's not hard to see *Edw'd de Vere* in there, is it? And what else can it mean?"

Oz thought about it between strokes, his skin glistening with sweat. He was so energetic that Hamish was finding it hard to keep up with him.

"Yeah, okay. I get that. It's pretty close, and he does seem to be trying to tell us something. Any more?"

Hamish stopped rowing and stood up. He was definitely out of training.

"Yes, here's a beauty. *The Winter's Tale* was given its rather odd title about that time. 'A Winter's Tale' would have been more natural. But guess what that is when translated into French? *Le Conte d'Hiver*. The Winter's Tale. And when de Vere visited the French court, what was he addressed as? Le Conte de Vere. Ha! Bingo! The sort of in-joke TB liked."

Oz stopped rowing and sat back, panting slightly. By now the sweat was pouring off him. He stood up and walked over to the weights while Hamish sat on a bench deciding on his next exercise.

"Wow, you've been doing your homework."

"Here's another," said Hamish. "Would you believe the word Vere actually crops up three times in *The Merry Wives*?"

"How did he manage that?"

"Dr Caius has a strong French accent, and is made to pronounce 'where' as 'Vere.' Clever, eh?"

"I like that one too," Oz admitted. "Yet another in-joke. Are you going for the weights?"

"No, I'm psyching myself up for the running machine. I need a bit of a jog. So you fancy my man de Vere for the post?"

"Let me see. Here's a test. The poet was lame, says so several times in the *Sonnets*. Does that work for de Vere?"

"Ha! Not a problem, chum. De Vere was badly wounded in the leg as a young man in a street fight with his mistress's uncle, and limped for the rest of his life. He refers to himself as 'a lame man' in a letter three years later. Good enough?"

"Give me one more," said Oz, when he'd lifted and put down a 45 lb weight. "One more and I'm over the hump."

"Well, would you believe a contemporary writer said of de Vere that 'he shaketh like a spere'. That was as close as he dared come to giving away his nom de plume. Will that do?"

"Right. It'll do for me," said Oz. "De Vere it is. I love that 'every word' thing. I'm going to have a shower, then I've got a fight call with all the gang. They're doing a full run through of the poisoning scene again, and I'm in it. Do you want to come? You could brush up your swordplay."

"Can't be bothered, frankly. I'm doomed to be just a bloody understudy all my life, let's face it. No, I'm only just starting to work up a sweat. I'll do another half an hour here, then I might pop in and see how you're all getting on. See you there."

35

A hit, a very palpable hit, I do confess it!
Act V, scene ii

Hamish left the basement gym and made his way up to the rehearsal room, pausing to exchange a word or two with people he passed. But as soon as he got there he could see something was wrong.

A little group was gathered round a figure lying on the floor, where the fight instructor knelt beside him. He raised his head as Hamish approached and called, "It's a nasty wound. Someone find the first aid kit. We've got to staunch the blood."

One of the actors left quickly to get assistance. Hamish could see Oz gripping his arm where blood was pouring out. The instructor started making a tourniquet as soon as a first aid box was produced. Oz saw Hamish and tried to grin. "What the hell, Oz...?"

Oz opened his mouth to reply but the actor playing Laertes turned to Hamish, spreading his hands, his eyes alarmed. "I don't really know what happened, Ham. We were just finishing a bout, and as I turned away, my foil went into Oz's arm. He must have been standing right behind me. The point's blunt of course, but at close range... it's obviously done quite a bit of damage."

Oz was waving further assistance away and speaking through gritted teeth.

"It's okay, darlings, it's under control. It'll stop bleeding in a minute. My own stupid fault. I was distracted by something, I don't know what. I just lost the plot for a moment and got in the way of the sword. I don't know what came over me - sorry, fans."

"Just keep still," ordered the instructor. "Keep your arm well up. Right, that should hold. Now go and sit down and someone will get you a cup of tea. Then we'll get you to A&E to have that seen to properly."

He straightened up. He was a muscular man with cropped grey hair, one of the best fight managers in the theatre business. He looked annoyed and worried at the same time.

"Okay everybody, that's it for the day. Another fight call tomorrow. And remember the lesson - these things are not toys."

Drama over, the actors began wandering away.

Hamish sat beside Oz on one of the chairs at the side of the room, and Oz put his head close to his.

"I'll tell you one thing," he whispered. "Ol's right. The Shadow really doesn't like us poking our noses in." He stared down at his arm, where a bright scarlet stain was spreading across the white fabric of the bandage.

"That's me done. I'm out of here. As far as I'm concerned, you can keep your bloody de Vere. Willy from Stratford wrote the plays, and that's how it's going to stay."

36

Speak the speech I pray, as I pronounced it to you,
trippingly, on the tongue
Act III, scene ii

"I love that funny face you make when you do your mouth," said Hamish. "But you are so much more beautiful before you whack all that shtick on, you know? *God has given you one face, and you make yourself another!*"

Olivia was hunched forward, peering into her dressing room mirror as she put the final touches to her make-up. "I think I'm getting a cold sore," she said. "That's all I need, along with the prospect of the Sir pawing all over me every night."

"Hey, tell him you're infectious. Got an STD! That should put him off!"

"Oh, come on, it is meant to be a love scene. Highly charged passion. We have to go through the motions." Olivia stood up.

"I know. But I should do it so much better than him, don't you think?" Hamish took her hands in an exaggeratedly theatrical pose. *"Lady, shall I lie in your lap?"*

"No, my lord," said Olivia, straightening her dress. "Shove off." *"I mean, my head upon your lap?"*

"Ay, good my lord."

"Did you think I meant... country matters?" Hamish pulled her to him and kissed her neck. "I rather like the sound of country matters, don't you?"

"I think nothing, my lord! Hey! You'll spoil my make-up, and curtain's up in twenty." She gave him a little kiss and pushed him away. "Are you sure Oz is all right? He's insisted on coming on tonight apparently."

"He'll be fine. It was only a flesh wound. Gave him a nasty fright though - he was talking about your Shadow."

"Told you he doesn't like us messing about, didn't I?" She shivered. "Polly stabbed in the arse - sorry, arras - Mr King poisoned in the orchard, and now Oz wounded in a sword fight. It'll be me next if I'm not careful." She put the finishing touches to her makeup, and straightened up. There was a *rat-a-tat-tat* as she did so, and one of the most famous faces in the theatrical world appeared round the door.

"Ah, my angel," said the Sir. "Sorry to barge in, darlings. Ooh, don't you look *gorgeous*. I just wanted to have one little word in your shell-like."

He was in full costume, in black from head to foot, his cropped fair hair bleached in contrast. Up close, you could see that his clothes were hanging loosely on him. He was reputed to be into heroin to keep his weight down, and his skin was in bad condition. He ignored Hamish for the most part and spoke only to Olivia.

"Do you mind if I give you the tiniest of notes? Just wondered whether you wanted to leave a *teeny-weeny* longer pause in the *O what a noble mind* speech? Just so the audience can appreciate what you're telling them about me. Do you remember I've mentioned it to you before? I know you young people don't study the iambic pentameter any more at drama school, but…"

Olivia opened her mouth to deny this vehemently, then closed it again. The Sir wandered over to her dressing table, picked up the copy of *HELLO!* that Olivia had been reading, and put it down again with a wince of distaste. The pupils in his eyes were like black olive stones, and Hamish could smell his acrid breath.

"I've been signing autographs outside. *What* a bore. These sad little people. What on earth do they do with my scrawls when they've got them, one wonders, in this amazing digital age of ours? They can't stick them in *albums* any more, can they? Oh, put them on Instagram or something I suppose, to impress their friends. Heaven give me strength."

His presence in the small room filled them with unease. As Olivia opened her mouth to speak, the muted chatter of the audience came over the loudspeaker. A metallic voice said, "*Ladies and Gentlemen of the Hamlet company, this is your fifteen minute call. Fifteen minutes please.*"

"And not *too* much cleavage, sweetheart. Delicious though your little dumplings are." He pressed a skinny finger onto her chest. Hamish felt himself growling like a dog straining at a leash but managed to say nothing. The Sir went on, "We don't want to distract the groundlings from the intricacies of the plot, now do we? That would never do. Well, we're on." He blew her a kiss and moved to the door.

"Good of you to drop in!" called Hamish. "Break a leg!"

There must have been an edge to his voice. The Sir froze, and turned round, his face scarlet. Hamish smiled sweetly at him, knowing he could hardly take exception to the time-honoured good luck wish of actors everywhere before going on stage.

The Sir stared at him.

"I know you think you would do the part so much better than me," he said. "Well, you're certainly pretty enough for it. A few more years' experience and hard slog and you never know, darling. Laters!" The door closed softly behind him.

There was a silence, and then Olivia exploded.

"*Well!* How dare he say that to you. What a bloody cheek! And I'll give him teeny pause."

"Teeny Paws? Sounds like a brand of cat food," said Hamish. "Spiteful old queen. He only wants to milk the audience for himself, that's all. Take no notice."

"Yes, and to put me in the shade more than ever! He already upstages me in every scene. Well, he can lump it. I'll chop the end off all his lines – see how he likes that."

"Sounds nice and painful," said Hamish. "Come on. *They are coming to the play. I must be idle.*"

"Let's hope it's a full house tonight for a change. *Good my lord, I come.*"

37

The play's the thing
Act II, scene ii

"The point envenomed too? Then venom, to thy work!"

The Sir's voice was cracking with passion. It was almost the conclusion of the final act. The audience were anticipating the climax of the play or the comfort of their own homes in equal measure. Apart from one interval, they had been nearly three hours in their seats.

The Sir stepped back from the dying Gertrude, and turned, half crouching, then springing, rapier raised, to stab Claudius. It was the height of the drama. At last Hamlet is to kill the King. But the Sir had failed to notice that the heavy poisoned goblet which the Queen had dropped had rolled across the stage, instead of falling down by her side.

The Sir stepped on the goblet, and shot across the full width of the stage, overbalancing as he went. The sword flew out of his hands and his arms flailed in the air like a threshing machine out of control. He cannoned full tilt into the sturdy wooden table, where the King and Queen were sitting to watch the fatal swordfight. The other actors watched horror-struck as his leg caught under the table, bending at an awkward angle as he fell.

The crack could be heard right across the auditorium.

The Sir gave a barely suppressed scream of agony and lay still, groaning. For a moment the scene was frozen as the actors stood transfixed. No-one knew what to do next. Horatio glanced around at the others, made an executive decision,. and stepped forward to bring the play to an abrupt end.

"Good night, sweet prince, and flights of angels sing thee to thy rest. The rest is silence," he cried. There was no applause from a stunned audience. Then the stage manager recovered from his disbelief and the huge curtains began to close ponderously across the set, concealing the horrific scene behind them.

Hamish went across to join Olivia, who had been standing in the wings with the rest of the cast waiting for the curtain call. Some of them looked shocked. Others had broad grins on their faces.

"Well, looking on the bright side," said Polly loudly, "Box Office shouldn't have to give any refunds. With a bit of luck nobody's going to notice a few lines missing from the end."

He turned to Horatio.

"Well done, Horesh. Best thing you could have done."

"Speak for yourself!" cried the tall man who was playing Fortinbras. "I've been waiting three hours to do my bloody lines. Never got to do my big speech tonight at all!"

The laughter grew louder, but stopped abruptly as a little procession of stagehands began carrying a prone figure on a stretcher. It was accompanied by Griselda, who had appeared from nowhere. She looked even whiter in the face than usual. The Sir was moaning feebly, blaspheming at every bump. As he was borne past Hamish, he fixed him with a piercing stare.

"Break a leg, eh?" he grated. "Well, I certainly did that, you little shit. I hope you'll have that on your conscience. Okay, it's your turn now. That'll be a laugh. *Ow!* Mind where you're going, you clumsy fools!"

Olivia squeezed Hamish's hand, and they watched in silence as the Sir was carried, cursing and wincing, into the wings. Griselda looked sharply back over her shoulder at Hamish as she followed the bearers, as if to put him on notice. Then they were gone.

"They bore him barefaced on a bier," Olivia whispered to Hamish, but he made no response. The actors in the wings had all fallen silent, their eyes on Hamish's face. It was his moment. He held his breath, his heart thumping. What were they thinking? Then Horatio called out, *"See, my lord! The election lights upon thee!* The part is yours!" He was grinning all over his face, genuinely pleased for his friend.

Now the others were clustering around Hamish, slapping him on the back, or shaking his hand.

You'll be terrific! Let's celebrate. You'll be much better than him. Who's buying the drinks? Did you see his face? Funniest thing ever seen at Stratford, God, I thought I'd die laughing. You're going to be fantastic.

Laughter was back in the air, and there was a palpable sense of relief among the company. Hamish's long period of waiting was over.

38

**And thus the native hue of resolution
Is sicklied o'er with the pale cast of thought,
And enterprises of great pith and moment
With this regard their currents turn awry**
Act III, scene i

Oz rang the doorbell of Polly's cottage. He was passing and, on an impulse, decided to call in. The street outside was as busy as ever with tourists and local people shopping, and the steps of the huge Art Deco theatre opposite had a constant flow of visitors in and out.

Polly opened the door with a frown. He was in his shirtsleeves, wearing a heavy pair of horn-rimmed glasses that Oz hadn't seen before. He peered over them at Oz, who was a fashion plate in his brightly-coloured silk shirt, white shorts and tiny straw hat, his arm in a black foam sling. Polly screwed up his eyes as if dazzled by the sun.

"Oh, it's you. What is it? I'm busy."

Oz wasn't fazed by this. Polly's truculence was notorious. He exaggerated his grumpy old man act, which gave him licence to bark offensively at people. Then he would suddenly disarm his victim with a grin as if to show that he was really a sweetie at heart and had just been pretending all the time. This little act fooled nobody.

"Looks like you could do with a break then. Got the coffee on?"

"I have as a matter of fact. How's the arm anyway?"

"Oh my God, the pain I was in. And did I get any sympathy? None at all." Oz sighed dramatically. He waited for a response from Polly, but, getting none, moved over the threshold. Polly had little option but to step back and allow him to enter. Books and paperwork were spread over the little table, on which a cigarette was burning on a full ashtray.

"What are you up to then, Polly? Looks interesting."

"Yesterday, I had Hamish round here telling me all about de Vere till my head was bursting. Then there was your ridiculous theory about the Fair Youth. Sometimes I wish I'd never said anything to any of you. I'm sick of the whole thing. But there was something about your idea that kept nagging me, and I've been running through it all to try and find the weakness."

Oz's face fell.

"And did you?"

"Oh yes. You may as well sit down, and I'll tell you. I have got some coffee percolating as it happens. Hang on. I'll get you a cup."

Polly was as fussy with his coffee as with his wines and came back shortly with a tray holding two china cups, Demerara sugar, a little silver jug of cream, and some madeleines on a side plate.

"It'll be ready in a minute."

Oz sat back on the cushions.

"Smells good. Well, let's hear it, sweetheart. My dreams of fame and fortune are disappearing in an aroma of a fine

Kenyan coffee, smelling faintly of pineapples. Am I right?"

"Well, you are about the coffee, as a matter of fact," admitted Polly grudgingly. "I don't know how you knew that."

"Oh, you're not the only person who knows his coffee, you know." Oz smiled keeping to himself his lucky guess that it was the same coffee Polly had served when they had come to dinner the night he was taken ill. Polly set his jaw.

"Okay, anyway I've been having a look at the dates as I said I would. We know that Will was born in Stratford in 1564, married Anne Hathaway in 1582 when he was 18. She was eight years older than him, and pregnant. She bore two more children in 1585, twins. Soon after this, he appears to have gone to London and found work as an actor."

"Okay, fine, Polly. He didn't fancy being a father of three, when he was barely past being a teenager and did a bunk to the big city. He won't have been the first. So, when were the sonnets written?"

"Probably between 1590 and 1605. They weren't published until 1609 though."

"And when did the Bard first start using the pseudonym *William Shake-speare?*"

"On three plays published in 1598."

Oz spread his hands.

"But those dates all work perfectly! Exactly as I've said!"

Polly didn't reply but got up and fetched the percolator from the tiny kitchen. He poured the dark liquid carefully into the delicate china cups. They both sipped appreciatively, and Polly lit a fresh cigarette.

"I know, but tell me this. If the Lovely Boy of the *Sonnets* is young Shaxpur from Stratters as per your theory, why does the Bard keep begging him to have children? The first seventeen sonnets are all on the same theme, beseeching him to get married. Like 'Sonnet 17', '*But were some child of yours alive that time, you should live twice; in it, and in my rhyme.*' To give just one example. But Will was already married and had three children by Anne Hathaway. Eh?"

Oz was stumped by this and scratched the back of his neck. "Hm... It hadn't occurred to me. I'll have to think about that."

"Yeah, you do. Knocks your precious theory sky high, I should say. All your dreams of fame and fortune gone." He grinned. "Sorry if I led you on a wild goose chase. But there you are, back to square one."

Polly seemed heartened by this idea, and his face had lost its strained look. In fact he was positively beaming. They called it *Schadenfreude*, thought Oz, someone taking pleasure in the misfortunes of others.

"No need to look so pleased. There could be half a dozen explanations," he said petulantly. "For a start, say he never told the Bard about his wife and kids in faraway Stratford? Perhaps they kinda slipped his mind? After all, he had escaped to London to forget them. Make a clean start. Maybe it wasn't something he wanted to broadcast. Didn't want to have spoilt his street cred with the other actors? Seems perfectly likely to me. He was the golden boy, the lovely youth. Anyway, his marriage was just a teenage indiscretion, best forgotten about. That's how he would have reasoned it." His voice had risen.

"All right," said Polly. "Keep your hair on. Just pointing it out. But I think it's a major stumbling block." He blew a perfect smoke ring, which floated out across the room for a moment before dispersing into thin air. Just like my Lovely Boy theory, thought Oz crossly.

Polly went on.

"Well, certainly nobody really understands that business about the Bard begging the young man in the *Sonnets* to father a child," he said. "Some people think he was writing to order for some reason. However – here's another thing." He picked up a sheet of paper with some notes on. "The *Sonnets* were published in 1609, with the mysterious dedication to a Mr W. H., the '*Onlie Begetter*'.

TO.THE.ONLIE.BEGETTER.OF.
THESE.INSVING.SONNETS.
Mʳ. W. H. ALL.HAPPINESSE.
AND.THAT.ETERNITIE.
PROMISED.

BY.

OVR.EVER-LIVING.POET.

WISHETH.

THE.WELL-WISHING.
ADVENTVRER.IN.
SETTING.
FORTH.

T. T.

Whether that means the writer or the person who inspired the *Sonnets*, a thousand scholars will argue about for a thousand days without finding the answer. Incidentally, the reference to 'our ever-living poet' in the dedication always refers to someone who is dead. Shaxpur was very much still alive and wasn't to die till 1616, but Ham's man de

Vere had died five years before the sonnets were published. I must admit that does seem to back your theory up." He looked over his glasses at Oz. "But leaving that aside, who do you suggest Mr W. H. was? Where does he fit into your equation? Answers on a postcard, please, as they used to say on the radio before you were born."

Oz helped himself to a madeleine, then stood up and looked out of the window at the scene on the grass running down to the river. A crowd of children were gathered round a fire eater dressed in Elizabethan costume. Won't be long before the Health and Safety Executive ban that, he thought moodily. He turned back to Polly.

"It should obviously read 'to Mr W. S.', referring to our boy from Stratford who did indeed beget the poems. I've no idea why it doesn't. It's the only explanation that really makes any sense. The poet is wishing all happiness and eternal life to the person who inspired him and whose name he took. But I have to admit it doesn't, so there it is," Polly said, carefully draining his coffee cup. "In fairness to you, a lot of people think that it is deliberate, a red herring to draw attention away from any hint of the writer's real identity. Or perhaps it was no more than a misprint. Representations of the letters 'S' and 'H' looked remarkably similar in Elizabethan calligraphy. They could easily have been mistaken by a busy printer copying from a manuscript. Bertrand Russell thought that."

"Bertrand who? Well, maybe. Now if I still had a picture of that bit from Pepys' diary, it might be a different matter. I would have some documentary proof." Oz laughed bitterly. "But with poor Mr King dead and the document now being firmly in the hands of his greedy brother, frankly I don't have a scrap of evidence. I'm even beginning to doubt it myself. So you needn't waste any more effort trying to convince me. It's been a lot of fun, but I'm going to move on. In more ways than one."

Polly laughed.

"Yes, from what you say that Pepys document is a ticking time bomb. If the brother ever releases the document to the press, it will put the cat properly among the pigeons, and maybe I'll enter the fray again... But that's for another day." He stood up and carried the remains of their coffee out to the kitchen.

Oz took this as a none too subtle signal to leave. He tightened the elaborate scarf around his neck and put his hat on. He followed Polly, who had already started piling the cups into the dishwasher.

"By the way, you want to know something? I wasn't really going to blow the gaff anyway. I'd decided against it, even before I got stabbed. It's not my job to ruin the pleasure of millions of people with a hypothesis that can't be proven. And before you start crowing too hard, may I remind you that it was you who sowed the seeds of doubt in me in the first place."

Polly shrugged as if to admit it, wiped his hands on a tea towel, and came over to the front door with him.

"You know, I think that's very wise," he said. "That was going to cause a whole lot of trouble for everyone concerned. Olivia will be very pleased, for one. I think she's right – the Bard doesn't want us to know too much. The total lack of material about his life makes that clear enough. Seems obvious to me that he destroyed all his papers before he died. Or that someone did it for him."

He opened the door for Oz. It was clear the visit was over. "Let's respect his memory and move on, before something worse happens to us. I think we're all agreed on that now, except Hamish, and he'll never make his mind up of course. Have you told him your decision yet?"

"No," said Oz, grimacing. "But I will, of course."

"You sound as if you've got plans?"

Oz breathed in the fresh scent of the river and the bouquet of the summer flowers across the road.

"Yes, I'm leaving the cast when the play transfers to London. Got a job in the States – L. A. actually. A friend of mine's got a luxury apartment in Beverley Hills, and he says there are loads of opportunities out there for a handsome talented thespian like me." He grinned and did a little mock modesty bow. "Expect to see me in Hollywood, Polly."

As they came out onto the doorstep, a passing couple looked at them. Oz guessed them to be American tourists, judging by their clothes. The man stopped abruptly and turned back. He peered at them closely, then nodded to himself.

"Pardon me interrupting you two genn'lmen," he said, "but my wife and I saw the show last night. Wunnerful stuff. Any chance of your autographs, if I may be so bold? To show the folks back home I've really been here? I have the programme in my pocket."

Polly shook his head without a word and simply closed the door to the cottage behind him. The tourist looked disbelievingly at the closed door. Oz smiled and took out his pen.

"My pleasure, sir. You have the programme?"

"Say, thanks. Here it is. Tell me something. Do you think Shakespeare would have known these very cottages when he was alive? Maybe wrote his plays on this very spot by the river?" said the man eagerly. He shushed his wife, who was making impatient noises.

"Bound to have done," said Oz, scribbling busily. "I don't doubt it for a moment. On this very spot."

"You hear that, Maudie?" The American was beaming all over his face. "We are standing in one of the most magical places on earth, sweetheart. Stratford-upon-Avon. Sir, you have truly made our day."

He clapped Oz on the back, and the couple moved down the riverside smiling contentedly. Stratford will never lose its magic, thought Oz, however many scholars debate however many theories. He grinned ruefully and set off to walk home.

39

The courtier's, soldier's, scholar's, eye, tongue, sword,
Th' expectancy and rose of the fair state,
The glass of fashion and the mould of form
Act III, scene i

Olivia smiled again as she watched from the wings, sipping a Coke from a can through a straw. It was a fine Saturday evening, and the house was full. Hamlet was taunting Polonius, walking towards him in a crablike motion.

"For yourself, sir, should be old as I am, if like a crab you could go backward."

The old man winced and turned away in a similar contortion, and the audience roared its approval.

It was less than a week since Hamish had stepped into the shoes of the Sir to take the eponymous role, but the mood in the theatre had completely changed. The other actors, the stage managers, the lighting crew, the programme sellers and even the bar staff were relaxed, smiling and cheerful with those around them. The house was packed night after night as the word had got round and there were none of those empty seats after the intervals which could be so dispiriting to the cast. Tickets were at a premium. Even Griselda was reported to have been glimpsed with an uncharacteristic smile on her face.

Hamish was a triumph in the part, and everyone acknowledged

it. The newspaper reviews were excited by the turn of events. *"A hit, a hit, I do confess it!"* said the Guardian. *"A star is born, yea, verily!"* said the Telegraph. The Stage thought it was *"An astonishing debut"*. Olivia shook her head in silent admiration as she watched Hamish move effortlessly from light-hearted banter to deeply introspective soliloquies, from playing the dilettante student, the *glass of fashion and the mould of form,* to the fighting man of action. The audience could rock with laughter at Hamlet's mischievous wordplay, then be moved to silence by his anguish at his father's death.

Now he was swapping sarcastic commentary with Rosencrantz and Guildenstern, now greeting the strolling Players as they arrived at the castle on their travelling stage.

"I am but mad north northwest," Hamlet told them. *"When the wind is southerly, I can tell a hawk from a handsaw."* The Players laughed uneasily, unsure of how serious he was, and the audience joined in. It was a *tour de force,* night after night, and Hamish was holding the house with a skill well beyond his years.

Olivia finished her drink and moved away. One of her play scenes was coming up and she needed some time to prepare herself. Every night was different, and there was little room for error in a production of such a high standard. She passed the Queen in the corridor. They paused for a moment.

"He's just amazing, isn't he?" said the Queen. "Such a breath of fresh air after that affected popinjay. So good to see a young man playing a young Hamlet for a change. Reminds me a little of dear Larry. You've got a star on your hands there, darling."

Olivia nodded.

"Certainly looks like it," she said, but to her annoyance heard a tiny voice inside herself piping, "Yes, but what about me?"

"Not that you're not a star too, my dear!" said the Queen just in time. "I so love your little Ophelia. Sheer magic." She smiled tightly. Close to, her face was very lined beneath the theatrical make-up. Olivia could never be quite certain whether fellow actors meant every word they said to each other about their performances, but she admired the Queen. She had been a very famous actress in her day, but that day was passing. This would be her last week on stage. Times were changing, and a younger, television actress had been cast to take over the part of Gertrude in the London production.

The Queen moved stiffly away, her hand trailing the wall for support, and Olivia watched her disappear round the corner. She was suddenly tired as well. It was nearly time for her entrance. It had been a long and demanding week. Thank God it was Sunday tomorrow.

40

Look here upon this picture, and on this
Act III, scene 4

"Mind you don't slip, sir. Deck's still wet from the rain last night."

Hamish nodded and extended a hand to Olivia, who passed him a small wicker hamper, then stepped daintily down into the little motorboat. She made a beautiful picture, Hamish thought. Her hair was tousled and highlighted by the sun, not by a hairdresser.

The boatman was standing in the shallows, holding the boat's painter fast with one hand and putting his other out for the fee. He had a swarthy complexion and a gold earring and would not have been out of place sailing with Sir Walter Raleigh in the sixteenth century.

"That's for three hours then, plus the deposit," he went on, in a strong Warwickshire accent. "An extra charge for every part of an hour that you're late back. Oh, and mind that patch of trees sticking out where the river bends a couple of miles on. Them willows can be treacherous. Folks have drowned there."

He spat a mouthful of chewing gum out into the river, pushing the cash into his back pocket and releasing the rope. Olivia looked sharply at him, wondering if the man was a secret playgoer with a wry sense of humour, who had recognized her as Ophelia, but dismissed the notion as fanciful. She had learnt that there was a section of Stratford's population which had little interest in the theatre.

Hamish was too busy fiddling with the controls to pay much attention. A couple of minutes later they were out in mid river, the water streaming off the bows catching the sunlight. The smell of the Avon, tangy and musty, filled their heads as the ducks quacked them goodbye.

They passed the stately bulk of the Royal Shakespeare Theatre. A few figures on the terrace looked down on them as they chugged past. A hand or two waved, and Olivia waved back. Then her eye was caught by the giant billboards outside the theatre.

"Look!" she cried. "They've put your face up next to mine! We're both on the billing now. Gazing into each other's eyes!"

"Don't you just love it!" said Hamish. "Fame at last! Now all we need is the fortune to go with it. Don't know about you, but I'm stony broke until the end of the month. But at least now I'm going to get a lot better paid for each performance." He seemed otherwise unmoved by his promotion to star status.

They grinned happily at each other. Olivia slipped out of her light jacket, exposing her bare arms, and leaned forward to kiss him. Hamish has become a different person in the last week or two, she thought. Confident and mature. A man with prospects even...

"Look out, Ol!"

She ducked, crouching like Hamish as the boat swept under a large overhanging branch. Prickly growths brushed their heads, but a few moments later they were clear of it, and burst out laughing.

"God, that nearly took my hair off, Ham!"

"Sorry, my fault. I steered too close to the bank. You leaning forward like that took my mind off the job."

Olivia made a baby face at him. A sudden plopping noise betrayed a large fish leaping up out of the water only yards away, shimmering twisting silver. Then all was quiet again. The sun was hot on their faces, and they could hear the tweeting of little birds in the bushes on the riverbank over the purr of the engine.

After twenty minutes, they were well away from the town and had the river to themselves.

"Turn the motor off, Ham," she said. "Let's just drift and listen to the sounds." Hamish obediently cut the engine, and the little boat was gently propelled downstream by the current. He got the oars out, and helped the boat down long reaches and round gently curving bends.

Time passed with a dreamlike quality. At first they didn't need to speak, content in each other's company and aware of the sounds of the river. Flies danced lazily over the water in the sunlight. But Olivia had something on her mind.

"Don't get excited, I haven't changed my mind about who wrote the plays. But just to satisfy my curiosity, can you sum it all up for my poor brain?"

"Just a sec. Don't want this lot in our propeller." Hamish steered adeptly round a floating patch of weed which was hovering in their path. Beyond that, the river ran clear and inviting. "Well, as far as I can gather, this is the scenario. The immensely erudite man of rank, Edward de Vere, who spent most of his life at the Royal Court, was the genius who wrote the sonnets and the plays. Everything we know about him - and that is a great deal - goes to show how well equipped he was to match the role. He had the education, the leisure, the experience, and the opportunity offered by his position. And so much of his life is mirrored in the plays, as must always be the case for any writer."

Hamish glanced back at Olivia. She was listening hard, a picture of young beauty in the sunlight against the background of the rippling water. Satisfied that he held his audience, he continued.

"For the first half of his career he wrote anonymously, probably under pressure from the Court, but also for other reasons relating to the dangerous political climate of the time. Although he married twice, he had a passionately homosexual side to his nature, and became besotted with a handsome young actor whom he met and worked with in the theatre. Most of his sonnets are addressed to this Fair Youth. His name, he tells us several times, was Will, and we say his surname was Shaxpur -- or Shagsper, or Shakspere, as it is variously spelt. By this time the poet was so successful that he simply had to choose a *nom de plume*. So he devised the name William Shake-speare, usually spelt with a hyphen, as a tribute to the young man, and used it ever afterwards. He tells us this in the sonnets."

"E'en as when first I hallowed thy fair name," mused Olivia dreamily, brushing away a little cloud of midges from around her hair. "Sorry - go on".

Hamish narrowed his eyes against the full sun as they rounded a wide bend.

"A lot of people must have been in the know, but the pseudonym had the backing of the Royal Court. It was more than anyone's life was worth to upset *them*. There are many hints about de Vere's real identity as the Bard, including some he couldn't resist dropping himself, but on the whole the pseudonym passed without comment."

"Then young Will got too cocky?"

"Yes indeed, and so he was given a substantial amount of money to leave London and go back home to Stratford. Which he did, although he returned to London from time to time, and among other transactions bought shares in the theatre. Again with financial assistance, no doubt."

Hamish stopped talking for a moment to negotiate a small bend, then continued.

"For several years, de Vere wrote his plays at white heat. But tragically, he died quite suddenly in 1604 at the age of fifty-four, of unknown causes. At that point, his personal history ends and he abruptly vanishes from the records of the period."

41

There is a willow grows aslant a brook,
That shows his hoar leaves in the glassy stream
Act IV, scene vii

Olivia was thoughtful as the boat proceeded up the river, its little engine hardly loud enough to disturb the midday peace.

"So what happened next?"

"There was a pause, but then the plays started to appear again and be performed. Incidentally, it is almost impossible to establish the dates the plays were written. There's an awful lot of guesswork involved. The last ones were incomplete or in draft form, and had to be edited by other leading playwrights of the day. These men were later described as collaborators, but of course they were no such thing." He paused for breath and to concentrate on steering.

"Finally in 1623 when the First Folio of the remaining plays was published, people started to want to know more about the writer."

"That's understandable." Olivia found herself nodding, thinking how much of the professional lecturer Hamish was revealing about himself. She was impressed, but tried not to show it.

"The man from Stratford had died in 1616, in possibly

dubious circumstances, his death unrecorded in London," he continued. "However, seven years later a tomb was erected in the church in Stratford, and the Shakespeare legend began to be kindled. The ubiquitous Ben Jonson had a hand in the inscriptions by the tomb, the publication of the Folio, and in Will's death. He'd been drinking with him the night before he died. Wow, look at him!"

A heron was rising noisily from a thicket on the nearside bank, looking for all the world like a broken umbrella blown by an invisible wind. They watched in silence as it flapped across in front of them to the other side of the river. Then Olivia said thoughtfully, "So the story of the man from Stratford being the playwright only began at that time?"

"Well, yes indeed, but not until well after his death, don't forget. Then over the centuries the legend grew and grew, becoming the billion pound industry we see today."

"Which has given untold pleasure to millions of people ever since, not to mention employment to us poor Thespians?"

"Absolutely."

"So why on earth would we want to promote our amateur and ill-informed theories and rain on everyone's parade?"

Hamish laughed.

"Can't argue with that. But you've got to admit it all falls into place now. The contradictions and the implausibility that have plagued scholars for years just disappear. What do you say? Are you sure you're not beginning to crack?"

Olivia didn't reply straight away. She set her jaw and was frowning, caught in a dilemma. Without warning a flash of orange, green and bright blue, a vision of dazzling colour, streaked just above the surface of the water, only to vanish as quickly as it had appeared. Their debate was forgotten in an instant.

"Wow, did you see that?" she cried. "A kingfisher! Wasn't that just beautiful?"

Hamish nodded, his eyes on the course ahead.

"There's always something to see on this river, isn't there? Did you know kingfishers close their eyes as they enter the water and catch the fish by smell?" he said.

You are as good as a chorus, my lord. I do hope you're not going to get boring in your old age." She was smiling now.

"Why should you care?" asked Hamish teasingly.

"Oh, I don't know. Just sorry for any poor girl that has to marry a know-all like you, that's all."

Hamish grinned.

"Why ruin a lovely day with dreary thoughts like that? Now why don't we stop and have our picnic. Make yourself useful and keep an eye out for a good spot on the bank to pull into. Hope you packed some wine?"

"Of course, silly. Great minds think alike. A bottle of Chardonnay. Doubt if Polly would approve of the vintage, let alone the screw top, but still. And some baguettes, butter, tomatoes, honey roast ham, English mustard. Oh, and some celery and boiled eggs. A flask of coffee for afterwards. And yes, I've brought some plastic cups. Bio-degradable, I need hardly add."

"Sounds pretty good to me. I'm starting the engine again now before we get marooned."

They drifted on down the river, lost again in wonder at its smells and sights. Hamish was standing up to steer, peering ahead like some intrepid explorer going up the Amazon. His skin was tanned against his sky-blue linen shirt, and he was humming a little tune. Olivia thought, don't let this day ever end.

42

But long it could not be
Till that her garments, heavy with their drink,
Pulled the poor wretch from her melodious lay
To muddy death.
Act IV, scene vii

As they rounded a bend, they came on a group of willow trees forming a haven in the crook of the river.

"Hello! This must be the place the boatman mentioned." Hamish eased back the throttle. A sandy inlet beside a tiny stream led to an open meadow behind the trees, where cows were grazing placidly. They raised their heads for a moment to gaze at the intruders, flies brushing their eyes.

"This looks like the perfect spot for our picnic though. What d'you reckon?"

"Go for it," said Olivia, though her voice quavered a little, and there was a strange feeling in the pit of her stomach. "It looks ideal. But be careful, Ham. You know what the man said."

Hamish skilfully negotiated their passage through the shade of the willow trees and into the little bay. He cut the engine and moored the boat to the branch of a tree, and they sat there for a moment in the silence, soaking up the peace. Olivia smiled uncertainly at him.

"There is a willow grows aslant a brook... I know," he said gently. He took her hand. "But I reckon you'll be safe enough as long as you don't start climbing out onto the branches and hanging fantastic garlands, don't you think?"

Somewhere in the distance was the sound of music, raucous and discordant. Where was that coming from?

"I will be safe as long as Oz has really given up the idea of making a fuss about his Lovely Boy theory," she said. "The Bard really doesn't like that, you know."

"Oh, I don't know," said Hamish. "I think I'm convinced. You've heard the whole thing. I'm pretty sure Oz is right actually. I can't see any holes in his argument about Shaxpur being the Lovely Boy, and I don't see why he shouldn't get the credit for discovering it."

Olivia sighed.

"Oh, Ham, darling!" she said, wanting very much not to get irritated. "You know that Oz has given the idea up after being stabbed. And I don't blame him and neither did you. Now you've changed your mind again. You really are the limit." She rose to pick up the hamper and put a leg out towards the bank. "I'm going ashore."

"Be careful," he said. "It's surprisingly deep just here. It's probably why they say it's dangerous."

Before she could answer, the peace was shattered. Round the bend came a motor launch carrying half a dozen people. They were gaudily dressed, and the women had stripped down to their bras in the hot sun. Empty wine bottles strewed the deck, and a radio was playing pop music loudly. The launch was travelling much too fast, and its wash had already reached the bank, crashing into the willows in wave after wave.

195

Olivia was poised between jumping on to the bank or stepping back into the boat as it rocked sharply up and down. She looked wild-eyed at the revellers, then cried out as she lost her balance and went into the water. She grabbed a low-lying branch, but it broke off. She went right under the surface and disappeared from sight. Hamish leant over the side but found he couldn't reach her. The boat was still rocking violently in the wake. He leapt to his feet and was in the water in a flash. Then he was beside her, trying to lift her out.

Try as he might, he couldn't move her, she was jammed under the keel by something unseen. She seized him fiercely round the neck in her panic and almost choked him as he struggled to lift her slender body. The weeping willow loomed down on to the river above them, brushing Hamish's head with its leaves in stately indifference.

He reasoned that her foot must be trapped by an underwater branch. He reached down to free it, gripping the side of the boat with his other hand to prevent it drifting downstream and marooning them. Now he could feel the obstruction, but he couldn't move it. He twisted at it, gasping with the effort, heaving as hard as he could but unable to shift it. Blind terror filled his heart.

Then without warning the obstruction came loose, making him stagger and nearly lose his footing. Olivia's foot had slipped out of its trap and she rose to the surface. She held on to Hamish's shoulders, sucking in great gulps of fresh air. He closed his eyes briefly in a silent prayer of thanks and dragged her on to the land. Her chest heaved up and down, and her eyes were half closed against the stinging water.

She coughed and spluttered, spewing out dirty river water.

Hamish left her to wade out to the boat again and seize the mooring rope, tying it quickly to one of the branches trailing in the water. As he did so the launch went past without slackening its speed. Its passengers were cheering and blowing a klaxon, offering vulgar suggestions before they turned a bend and went out of sight.

Hamish stared after them in disbelief, then turned to Olivia. "Are you hurt?" he asked, his arm round her shoulders. "Oh my God... those bastards."

Olivia slowly sat up, her chest still heaving, and looked down at her leg which was streaming with blood.

"Scraped it on the side of the boat as I went in. My foot's scratched, that's all," she said breathlessly. She touched the wound and gasped, wincing. Then without warning she was consumed with rage.

"Do you see what you've done now, with your damned theories?" she shouted. "This isn't funny! I nearly died! I'm not joking about this Shadow thing, you know. And neither is he!"

"I know, darling," said Hamish, taken aback by her uncharacteristic show of temper. "That was bloody dangerous, all right. Fools. Bastards. Stupid drunken bastards. People like that shouldn't be on the river. I'll report them when we get back. I'll... Okay, I'm going to get the rug and wrap you up." He climbed back into the boat, and was back in a moment with the picnic basket and the rug which he wrapped round her shoulders.

They sat quietly in the sun, its warmth gradually restoring their spirits. They both had little to say, shocked and scared by the turn of events. After a while, they began to feel more normal. Hamish stood up.

"Do you feel up to something to eat? Might cheer us up."

Olivia smiled feebly.

"Thank you. That would be very nice. Sorry I shouted at you. I will have something. But no wine, yet please. I'm still feeling a bit sick."

Her wet top and shorts had dried quickly in the hot sun. They opened the basket and spread out the contents on a grass a little way from the river, glad of something to do. The food and wine went some way towards reviving them both, although neither had much of an appetite, and soon they got back in the boat and set off back home.

43

Good night, sweet Prince.
And flights of angels sing thee to thy rest
Act V, scene ii

The return journey was much more subdued than the outward voyage.

"Tell me something," said Olivia, breaking the silence. She trailed her hand in the water as the boat puttered steadily up the river. "Now do you think I'm just being silly when I say that Shakespeare's Shadow doesn't like people questioning his identity?"

Hamish was intent on steering and made no reply.

"You must admit there have been some very nasty incidents since Polly and Oz came up with the Lovely Boy theory. A stabbing, the poisoning in your dream, poor Mr King, of course, Oz's fencing accident, and now the willows, where I nearly paid the ultimate price for your cynicism. Is that a fair assessment?"

"It does all seem a bit odd when you look back on it," said Hamish, carefully negotiating a log covered with vegetation which was sailing sedately towards them midstream. "And obviously they all mirror nasty accidents that happen to the characters in *Hamlet*. Is that a crocodile? God, it really looks like one. Okay, I must admit I've been pretty convinced by

Oz's case at times. Especially the *Sonnets* about hallowing his sweet name. And de Vere's life is such a good fit. But okay, after this I feel like putting the whole idea behind us. You were nearly drowned. Polly's had a scare and learnt his lesson. And Oz has had a sudden change of mind and is off to forget all about it in sunny California."

"Poor Oz. Can't say I blame him. That was a nasty wound he had."

They were approaching Stratford now. There was distant music in the air from the bandstand, and a first few adventurous ducks appeared, pecking along the bank for food.

Hamish smiled at her.

"Okay, I surrender. I say good for you, Will. As long as your wonderful words live on, your secret's safe with us. If you're hiding something, you've made it pretty clear you don't want us to know what. You've had the last laugh."

Exactly on cue, a mallard with exceptionally beautiful green and black colouring let out a loud and raucous cackle of laughter which racketed across the river. *Quack quack quack quack quack.*

"He certainly has!" Olivia giggled. "You can say that again. Good luck, old Shadow!"

The two young people rounded the bend to the little town, its theatres prominent as they approached. The big billboards with their own giant faces quickly became visible, heralding a golden future for them. Beside them another large notice advertising the alternative production spelt out its own message.

"ALL'S WELL THAT ENDS WELL," it loudly proclaimed.

They looked at each other and burst into laughter again.

With the resilience of youth, their good spirits were restored. Olivia looked around as they approached the quayside, her hand round Hamish's waist. Beyond the theatre the cumulonimbus clouds had piled up, painting pictures in the sky.

One cloud stood out against the rest. Olivia stared. Wasn't that Shakespeare's image high about the theatre? Yes, there was his bald head, and the familiar ruff and doublet. She pointed up excitedly and squeezed Hamish's arm.

"Look! There he is!" she cried. "Can you see him? He's happy now. Shakespeare is Stratford and Stratford is Shakespeare. And always will be."

And as puffs of cloud drifted lazily across the blue sky above the Avon, like balls of cotton wool, the Bard winked.

Thanks to my partner Barbara James for her patience and invaluable assistance, to Lin O'Donnell for her expert editing advice, and to Derek Johnson for his technical support and more. Thanks to Philip and Suzy Marvin for their Italian seminar on Hamlet, and to Katie Gabriel Allen for her invaluable and unexpected publishing skills as well as her lovely cover artwork, and to Sue Cowap for her technical and moral support.

For more about my books, do visit my <u>author website</u>: <u>https://vaughandavies.org/</u> and my Facebook page @RichardVaughanDavieswriter

HAMLET – the play
by William Shake-speare

For readers who are unfamiliar with this wonderful play, or perhaps retain only a dim recollection of it from their schooldays, the following abridged summary may help to throw light on some of the events in the novel. Loose associations with the plot may be detected from time to time.

Hamlet, Prince of Denmark, is romantically involved with Ophelia, but denies he loves her. Having been summoned home to attend his father's funeral, he is shocked to find his mother Gertrude already remarried. The Queen has all too swiftly married Claudius, the dead king's brother.

When his father's ghost appears, Hamlet's suspicions are confirmed. The Ghost tells him that Claudius poured poison into King Hamlet's ear while the old king slept in his orchard. He implores Hamlet to avenge his murder.

Hamlet is very indecisive. In his continued reluctance to dispatch Claudius, he actually causes several related deaths. The first death is that of Ophelia's father Polonius, whom Hamlet stabs through an arras, a hanging curtain. Claudius then sends for Hamlet's so-called friends Rosencrantz and Guildenstern, and he instructs them to despatch Hamlet to execution.

Ophelia, distraught over her father's death and Hamlet's behaviour, drowns in the river by the willows. Her brother Laertes plots with Claudius to kill Hamlet. In a sword fight, attended by the courtier Osric, Hamlet retrieves the poisoned sword and cuts Laertes. Because Hamlet has already been wounded with the same sword, he too will die. Gertrude has drunk a toast to her son from the poisoned cup Claudius had intended for Hamlet and dies.

Finally resolved to action, Hamlet stabs Claudius with the poisoned sword and pours the last of the poisoned wine down the King's throat. Hamlet's last words are: "The rest is silence."

WILLIAM SHAXPUR - Timeline

1564 William Shakspere (sic) born in Stratford-upon-Avon (26 April)

1582 William Shaxpere (sic) marries Anne Hathaway

1583 Daughter Susanna born

1585 Twins Judith and Hamnet born

1587 Around this time, WS leaves Stratford to be an actor in London. (Next seven years unknown, possibly working as an actor)

1592 First (possible) reference to WS in print *('an upstart Crow the only shake-scene')* in Robert Greene's pamphlet, *A Groats-worth of Witte*

1593 Plague closes London theatres.

      William Shakespeare (sic) (first use of the name) publishes two narrative poems, 'Venus and Adonis' and 'The Rape of Lucrece', both dedicated to the Earl of Southampton

1595 The Chamberlain's Men are formed and frequently perform at the court of Elizabeth I

1596 Hamnet dies aged 11

1597 WS buys New Place, Stratford-upon-Avon

1599 Many of Shakespeare's most famous plays are performed for the first time at the Globe Theatre, a wooden theatre built by The Lord Chamberlain's Men. The plays include

Hamlet, Othello, and King Lear. Plays believed to have been written in 1599 include As You Like It and Julius Caesar, *the first known WS play to be performed at the Globe Theatre*

1601 Burial of WS's father, John Shakspeyr (sic)

1603 The Chamberlain's Men become The King's Men after the death of Elizabeth 1 and the accession of James I

1607 WS's daughter Susanna marries John Hall, physician
The King's Men begin playing at the Blackfriars (indoor) Theatre in the winter and the Globe Theatre in the summer

1608 WS's mother (Mary née Arden) dies

1609 'Shakes-peares *Sonnets*' (sic) are published

1616 On 25 March, William Shakspere (sic) makes his will

1616 WS dies, and is buried on 25 April

1623 First Folio, *Mr William Shakespeares Comedies, Histories, & Tragedies*, published by two of Shakespeare's fellow actors/ friends, John Heminge and Henry Condell. The Folio starts with a verse, 'To the Reader', by writer Ben Jonson.

Without the First Folio, many of Shakespeare's plays might not have survived

1623 A monument to Shakspeare (sic) is erected in Holy Trinity Church, Stratford-upon-Avon

Variants on his name

William Shaxpere of Stratford upon Avon is the name as it appears in his marriage licence. Other versions over the period include:

Shakespere, Shackspeare, Shakespear, Shakspere, Shaxspere, Shaxper, Shakspeare, Shackespeare, Shackspere, Shackespere, Shakespere, Shackspeare, Shakespear, Shakspere, Shaxspere, Shaxper, Shakspeare, Shackespeare, Shackspere, Shackespere (but never Shakespeare or Shake-speare)

EDWARD DE VERE - Timeline

1550 *April 12* Edward de Vere (EV) is born at Castle Hedingham, Essex.

1562 *September 3* His full title from now on would be – Edward de Vere, 17th Earl of Oxenford, Lord Great Chamberleyn of England, Viscount Bulbecke, and Lord of Badlesmere and Scales. He generally signed his letters 'Edward Oxenford', with the additional flourish of an Earl's coronet.

1564 Cambridge University: EV is awarded an honorary degree of MA.

1566 Oxford University: EV is awarded an honorary degree of MA.

1567 EV is admitted to Gray's Inn to study Law.

1567 EV accidentally kills William Cecil's undercook while practising his fencing. He is acquitted and goes unpunished.

1570 EV enlists with the Earl of Sussex for the Scottish military campaign.

1571 EV is described as an up-and-coming star of Elizabeth I's court.

1571 *December* EV marries Anne, daughter of Lord Burghley, Lord Treasurer. (*Cf. Hamlet and Ophelia*.)

1572 EV writes the preface in Latin to Castiglione's *Il Cortegiano* (*The Courtier*).

1573 EV's servants are accused of waylaying travellers on the Gravesend-Rochester road. (*Cf. Act II, Scene 2 in Henry IV', Part 1 in which Falstaff and companions rob travellers, carrying the King's taxes, on the same road*).

1574 EV heads for the continent. He visits Flanders, Strasburg, Padua, Venice, Florence, Verona, Siena and Sicily, and stays several months in Italy, forming a strong attachment to the country. Many of Shakespeare's plays are later based on the Italian tradition of *La commedia dell'arte*.

1575 In a letter to Burghley from Paris, EV thanks him for the information about his wife Anne being pregnant: '*then perhaps I will bestow two or three months to see Constantinople, and some part of Greece.*'

1575 *April* EV travels to Strasburg where he meets Sturmius.

1575 *July 2* Anne (née Cecil) gives birth to a daughter.

1575 *Nov 27* A letter from EV to Burghley from Padua.

1576 *Jan 3* A letter from EV to Burghley from Siena, opens: '*My lord, I am sorrie to hear how hard my fortune is in England*'.

1576 Burghley is worried that his son-in-law EV will not accept paternity of his daughter, Anne's child.

1576 *March* EV arrives in Paris on the way home to England.

1576 *April* Crossing from France to England, EV's boat is attacked by Dutch pirates who loot most of his possessions. (*Cf. 'Hamlet's misadventure at sea'.*)

1576 Back in England, EV writes to Burghley saying he

has no intention of meeting up with his wife.

1578 EV invests in Frobisher's disastrous second voyage to seek out a Northwest passage.

1578 EV is eulogised by Cambridge scholar Gabriel Harvey as a prolific poet and as one whose '*countenance shakes speares.*'

1580 EV is caricatured as an 'Italianate Englishman'. He is also praised as '*peerless in England as a discourser for tongue*', i.e. a linguist.

1581 *23 March* The unmarried Anne Vavasour, one of the Gentlewomen of the Queen's Bedchamber, gives birth to a son who would be named Edward Vere. EV was known to be the child's father and is sent to the Tower.

1581 *9 June* EV is released from the Tower and placed under house arrest in Greenwich.

1582 *January* Reconciliation between Anne (née Cecil) and EV.

1582 *March* In a 'fray' between EV and Sir Thomas Knyvett, EV is injured, making him lame for the rest of his life. (*Cf. references to the poet's lameness in the 'Sonnets'.*)

1582 EV's brother-in-law, Lord Willoughby is made Ambassador to the Danish court at *Elsinore*.

1583 EV's newly born son by Anne dies.

1583 EV acquires the sub-lease on the Blackfriars Theatre and appoints his secretary Lyly as manager.

1584 Daughter Bridget born to EV and Anne.

1584 EV acquires the London mansion known as Fisher's Folly which becomes the centre of his literary salon.

1586 Privy Seal Warrant from the Queen granting EV £1,000 p.a.

1586 EV described by William Webbe a *'most excellent'* among court poets.

1587 *May* Daughter Susan born to EV and Anne.

1587 *Sept* Daughter Frances dies in infancy.

1588 *June* EV's wife Anne (Cecil) dies and is buried in Westminster Abbey.

1588 EV fits out his ship the *Edward Bonaventure* against the Spanish Armada and is described as having stood *'like warlike Mars upon the hatches'*.

1589 *'Now are sprung up another crew of Noble men and Gentlemen of her Majesties own servants, who have written excellently, of which number is first that noble Gentleman Edward Earle of Oxford.'* The Art of English Poesie.

1591 EV marries Queen Elizabeth's Maid of Honour, Elizabeth Trentham.

1591 EV sells the manor of Castle Hedingham, the de Vere family seat from the time of William the Conqueror, to Lord Burghley, in trust for his daughters Elizabeth, Bridget and Susan.

1593 Henry de Vere, son of EV and Elizabeth (née Trentham) is born.

1595 EV's daughter Elizabeth marries the sixth Earl of Derby, who maintains his own company of players. The festivities are concluded with a performance of *A Midsummer Night's Dream*.

1596 Dedicatory verse to EV in Spenser's *Faerie Queene*.

1597 *September 2* EV and his wife purchase King's Place in Hackney, a substantial country manor house with a Great Hall, a classic Tudor Long Gallery, a chapel and '*a proper librayre to lay books in*'; the land comprising around 270 acres of farmland. It would remain their principal London home until EV's death in 1604.

1598 EV is named as 'best for comedy' in Francis Meres' *Palladis Tamia*.

1603 *Mar 24* Queen Elizabeth dies, succeeded by James I.

1603 EV's Crown annuity is renewed by King James. He refers to EV as '*Great Oxford*'.

1604 King James grants EV custody of the forest of Essex and the Keepership of Havering, and he is reappointed to the Privy Council.

1604 *June 24* EV dies, aged 54, of unknown causes.

1604 *July 6* EV is buried at St John's Church, Hackney. There was little ceremony, and thereafter historical mention of him ceases abruptly.

SHAKE-SPEARES

SONNETS.

Neuer before Imprinted.

AT LONDON
By *G. Eld* for *T. T.* and are
to be solde by *William Aspley.*
1609.

Sonnet 36

Let me confess that we two must be twain,
Although our undivided loves are one
So shall those blots that do with me remain
Without thy help, by me be borne alone.
In our two loves there is but one respect,
Though in our lives a separable spite
Which though it alter not love's sole effect,
Yet doth it steal sweet hours from love's delight.
I may not evermore acknowledge thee,
Lest my bewailed guilt should do thee shame,
Nor thou with public kindness honour me,
Unless thou take that honour from thy name:
But do not so; I love thee in such sort
As, thou being mine, mine is thy good report.

Sonnet 55

Not marble nor the gilded monuments
Of princes, shall outlive this powerful rhyme;
But you shall shine more bright in these contents
Than unswept stone, besmeared with sluttish time.
When wasteful war shall statues overturn,
And broils root out the work of masonry,
Nor Mars his sword nor war's quick fire shall burn
The living record of your memory.
'Gainst death and all-oblivious enmity
Shall you pace forth; your praise shall still find room
Even in the eyes of all posterity
That wear this world out to the ending doom.
So, till the Judgement that yourself arise,
You live in this, and dwell in lovers' eyes.

Sonnet 73

That time of year thou mayst in me behold
When yellow leaves, or none, or few, do hang
Upon those boughs which shake against the cold,
Bare ruin'd choirs, where late the sweet birds sang.
<u>In me thou see'st the twilight of such day</u>
As after sunset fadeth in the west,
Which by and by black night doth take away,
Death's second self, that seals up all in rest.
In me thou see'st the glowing of such fire
That on the ashes of his youth doth lie,
As the death-bed whereon it must expire,
Consum'd with that which it was nourish'd by.
This thou perceiv'st, which makes thy love more strong,
To love that well which thou must leave ere long.

Sonnet 76

Why is my verse so barren of new pride,
So far from variation or quick change?
Why with the time do I not glance aside
To new-found methods, and to compounds strange?
Why write I still all one, ever the same,
And keep invention in a noted weed,
That every word doth almost tell my name,
Showing their birth, and where they did proceed?
O know, sweet love, I always write of you,
And you and love are still my argument;
So all my best is dressing old words new,
Spending again what is already spent:
For as the sun is daily new and old,
So is my love still telling what is told.

Sonnet 81

If I shall live your epitaph to make,
Or you survive when I in earth am rotten;
From hence your memory death cannot take,
Although in me each part will be forgotten.
Your name from hence immortal life shall have,
Though I, once gone, to all the world must die:
The earth can yield me but a common grave,
When you entombed in men's eyes shall lie.
Your monument shall be my gentle verse,
Which eyes not yet created shall o'er-read,
And tongues to be your being shall rehearse,
When all the breathers of this world are dead;
You still shall live, such virtue hath my pen,
Where breath most breathes, even in the mouths of men.

Sonnet 95

How sweet and lovely dost thou make the shame
Which, like a canker in the fragrant rose,
Doth spot the beauty of thy budding name!
O! in what sweets dost thou thy sins enclose.
That tongue that tells the story of thy days,
Making lascivious comments on thy sport,
Cannot dispraise but in a kind of praise;
Naming thy name, blesses an ill report.
O! what a mansion have those vices got
Which for their habitation chose out thee,
Where beauty's veil doth cover every blot,
And all things turn to fair that eyes can see!
Take heed, dear heart, of this large privilege;
The hardest knife ill-used doth lose his edge.

Sonnet 108

What's in the brain that ink may character,
Which hath not figur'd to thee my true spirit?
What's new to speak, what new to register,
That may express my love or thy dear merit?
Nothing sweet boy; but yet, like prayers divine,
I must, each day say o'er the very same;
Counting no old thing old, thou mine, I thine,
<u>E'en as when first I hallow'd thy fair name.</u>
So that eternal love in love's fresh case,
Weighs not the dust and injury of age,
Nor gives to necessary wrinkles place,
But makes antiquity for aye his page;
Finding the first conceit of love there bred,
Where time and outward form would show it dead.

Sonnet 135

Whoever hath her wish, thou hast thy *Will,*
And *Will* to boot, and *Will* in over-plus;
More than enough am I that vex thee still,
To thy sweet will making addition thus.
Wilt thou, whose will is large and spacious,
Not once vouchsafe to hide my will in thine?
Shall will in others seem right gracious,
And in my will no fair acceptance shine?
The sea, all water, yet receives rain still,
And in abundance addeth to his store;
So thou being rich in *Will* add to thy *Will*
One will of mine, to make thy large Will more.
Let no unkind, no fair beseechers kill;
Think all but one, and me in that one Will.

***In the Shadow of Shakespeare* is a work of fiction**. But over the years, many have theorised about the identity of the Bard. Some of the greatest minds who have studied Shakespeare's works have harboured doubts about the writer's identity. In his 1613 play, *The Revenge of Bussy D'Ambois*, poet George Chapman identifies Edward de Vere, Earl of Oxford, as responsible for Shakespeare's plays and sonnets. This was while William Shaxpur was still alive.

The famous founder of psychoanalysis, Sigmund Freud, who used Shakespeare's plays to build his theories on, says in his *An Autobiographical Study* (1927):

"I no longer believe that William Shakespeare the actor from Stratford was the author of the works that have been ascribed to him."

For more information on the subject, you can visit the website of The Shakespeare Authorship Coalition (https://doubtaboutwill.org/) where you will also be able to read 'The Declaration of Reasonable Doubt'. This is a superb summary of the issue, expressed in mild and reasonable terms.

The De Vere Society (https://deveresociety.co.uk), is dedicated to Edward de Vere, the Earl of Oxford, saying, "De Vere, or not De Vere? That is the question..."

On their website, you will also find links to other organisations such as The Shakespearean Authorship Trust, and the Shakespeare Oxford Fellowship.

RECOMMENDED READING

Anderson, Mark – *Shakespeare By Another Name*

Bryson, Bill – *Shakespeare*

Casson, John, and Rubinstein, William D. – *Sir Henry Neville was Shakespeare*

Chambers, G.K. – *William Shakespeare: A Study of Facts and Problems* (2 volumes)

Edmondson, Paul – *Shakespeare Beyond Doubt* [see Shahan and Waugh, below]

Freud, Sigmund – *An Autobiographical Study*

Green, Alan William – *Dee-Coding Shakespeare*

James, Brenda, and Rubinstein, William D. – *The Truth Will Out*

Michell, John – *Who Wrote Shakespeare*

Nield, Robert – *Breaking the Shakespeare Codes*

Ogburn, Charlton – *The Mysterious William Shakespeare*

Pepys, Samuel – *The Diary of Samuel Pepys*

Pointon, A J – *The Man Who Was Never Shakespeare*

Price, Diana – *Shakespeare's Unorthodox Biography*

Shahan, John, and Waugh, Alexander – *Shakespeare Beyond Doubt?*

Shapiro, James – *A year in the life of William Shakespeare: 1599*

Twain, Mark – *Is Shakespeare Dead?*

Whittemore, Hank – *100 Reasons Shake-speare was the Earl of Oxford*

Winchcombe, George and Bernard – *Shakespeare's Ghost Writer(s)*

*If you have enjoyed this, we feel sure you will also enjoy
Richard Vaughan Davies's earlier novel*

IN THE SHADOW OF HITLER

1

Hamburg, 1946

"Right. That's more than enough for one day. I'm off. See you tomorrow, Pinkie."

The door opens onto the black moonscape of the ruined street. I am only inches away from dirty snowflakes tearing down the road in great swirling clusters, like dust motes under the broom of an unseen giant.

I'm stiff and tired. There is just so much of man's inhumanity to man that you can take. I have reached that limit, and am ready for home.

Pinkerton looks up at me and through me, running his ink stained fingers distractedly through his thinning hair. He's definitely going bald. He is beginning to get round shouldered too, and some days looks more like a man of sixty than thirty. He has rolled up his shirtsleeves, though the room is warmed only by a one- bar electric fire, and is peering through his wire rimmed glasses at a closely typed document. A pot of ink and a half-drunk mug of coffee stand at his elbow.

"Righty-ho," he says absently. "Oh - better check the doors, will you, Adam? Caretaker's not shown up again. Second time this week."

"It's this 'flu that's going round. Helga's off as well."

My highly efficient secretary, she of the elaborate hairdo and muscular legs, is prone to sudden inexplicable bouts of illness which necessitate her staying at home. They sound life threatening when she reports them, although she always manages to turn up unscathed the next day for work with the briefest of explanations.

"Adam?"

"Pinkie?"

I am not in the mood for a long conversation.

"Can you answer me something? It's important. It's ridiculous, I know, but tell me truthfully – what's your guess of how many camps there were? Concentration camps I mean, obviously. Any idea?"

Pinkie stares at me, pen tapping his teeth. He looks exhausted.

I'm poised awkwardly by the door. I've only popped into his office to say goodnight from a different part of the building where I work. The weather's awful, and I'm freezing just standing here. But I can see that he needs an answer, and attempt to give one.

"Well, I used to just know about the big ones," I say slowly. "Then we realised there were a lot more than we first thought. We're finding more all the time, aren't we? I don't know really, Pinkie. I've only been concerned with the one at Scheiden really."

I shudder suddenly, I suppose because of the hail rattling at the window. It's getting dark now. The roofless warehouse opposite, with huge gaping holes in its walls, is turning into a grotesque face. It seems to grin at me as it merges into the shadows like a Cheshire cat.

"So...?"

Pinkie prompts me.

"Well – with Poland and so on as well, I suppose... what, fifty, a hundred even? More? Don't tell me – more?"

He puts his pen down and stares out at the wintry scene outside his window.

"I've listed seven hundred now, and there are others coming to light every day. It looks certain there were literally thousands of them. It's quite unbelievable."

"Thousands? Good God Almighty!" I feel as if I've had a blow to the solar plexus. "What? Are you serious?"

Pinkie turns his almost comically worried face to me.

"Okay, I'm not talking about extermination camps, with gas ovens and so, where prisoners only lived a few hours after arrival. There were a certain number of those, I don't know how many yet. I'm talking about KLs, detention camps. They had a staggeringly high death rate too. Do you know what? It seems likely to me that every town in the country of any size at all had one of these located nearby. I'm not exaggerating. Every one. And yet nobody saw a darned thing."

"Yes. Yes, I know."

"And yet we're supposed to work with these people every day."

He was almost shouting. "And treat them like colleagues. I tell you, Adam, sometimes it makes me want to be sick."

I swallow hard. There's a point of view I want to put, and I don't know really why. Perhaps it's because I've learnt surprisingly quickly to regard many German people as my friends and not as my enemies.

"That's unbelievable. But be honest, Pinkie. Would the average Briton be any different, really? We're talking about human nature. We only see what we want to see? Don't we?"

But I've learnt from experience that this is not a popular opinion, and Pinkie isn't in the mood to hear my amateur philosophizing. He cuts me off with a wave of his hand. For my part I don't want an argument either, so I walk over and put my arm round his thin shoulders. I give him a brief hug, conscious that it is a very un-English thing to do.

"Good night, old man. Illegitimi non carborundum, or words to that effect."

He manages a weak smile.

"Don't let the bastards grind you down, eh? Well, one can but try."

"That's the spirit. Good night, then. I'm off."

He just grunts, and sits down again to his files.

"Oh, and Pinkie...?"

"What?"

"That's your coffee cup you've just put your pen in."

Pinkie blinks at it myopically.

"Oh, drat. I seem to do that sometimes."

He reaches in his pocket and pulls out a cotton handkerchief to wipe the pen clean.

"Stupid. Makes the very dickens of a mess."

"Pinkie, don't you think it's time you packed it in and went home?"

"Oh, yes, yes. I will in a while. Just got to finish this thing for Foxy."

I had an inspiration.

"Look here, do you fancy a drink? Apparently there's a new

bar of sorts opened near where the fish market was. Dancing and so on. Sounds quite interesting."

He bends over his desk again and peers myopically down at his document. "I'd love to, Adam. I would really, but not this evening. Another time perhaps."

"Another time then."

It's a bit difficult to imagine Pinkie dancing the night away. I grin to myself and go out into the night.

It has stopped snowing, but the uneven pavements are slippery as I leave the warmth of the Kriegskriminalanlage office behind, hunching my shoulders against the chill. The cold wind they say comes from Russia stings my cheeks as I cut through the remains of the old Pilsnauerpark into the darkened side streets and turn off Feldhausweg towards home, picking my way carefully through the ruins.

In parts of the city, the whole street system has disappeared. People who were born here and have worked here all their lives can no longer find their bearings. Huge piles of rubble, concrete and collapsed or derelict buildings are the new landmarks to be negotiated, where once stood houses and the shops inhabited by industrious housewives and tired clerks, noisy children and grumbling grandparents. Winding cobbled lanes, with black and white half-timbered medieval houses huddling side by side had survived the Plague and the Black Death, but almost overnight vanished forever. The delicately wrought stained glass windows, soaring roofs, and finely sculpted arches of ancient churches are now just piles of stones and blackened beams.

Broken buildings tower everywhere against the evening sky, mute in their misery. Across the whole city the many canals are still unusable, blocked with debris. Weeds grow rampant in the rubble and I have become grateful for them. Their purple, yellow, blue and scarlet flowers provide a relief to the black, charred landscape of the burnt out cityscape. But their flowers are dying now as winter approaches, and their stems, bending against the hail, are hard to make out in the gloom.

Street lighting exists no more, and the only illumination comes from the eerie glow of bonfires and braziers on the sites of bombed out buildings, where hundreds of the homeless have made shelters in the ruins. Dwellings for entire families, some surprisingly elaborate, are provided by the remains of the buildings and cellars of the houses and shops which line the once elegant streets.

In this part of the city, in some streets only fragments of buildings have survived the last days of the American and British saturation bombing, but even these provide some sort of shelter. I often pass grubby children playing merrily on the piles of rubble, sometimes acting out the actions of the planes and the noise of the bombing.

The aftermath of the holocaust is all around me. In the final days of the endless bombardment the bombing created an enormous firestorm, which sucked out the air and raised the temperature to over a hundred degrees, suffocating to death thousands who until then had thought they had survived. I grit my teeth when I recall that, almost unbelievably, the Allied bombing resumed the following day, seeking to extinguish even such sparks of life that still remained. But the bombers turned away one by one. There was nothing left to destroy.

Yet a kind of miracle has occurred. Slowly, timidly, life has returned, inch by inch, breath by breath. And now, over a year since the war ended, defeat acknowledged, and a surrender signed by the broken survivors, an urban society is re-establishing itself. Food is still scarce, but mass starvation has been overcome, and fuel is becoming easier to get hold of. There is a living to be made by the able bodied, salvaging timber from the thousands of bomb sites and selling it for firewood. The old opencast coal workings near Thorsburg have been reopened too, and coal carts, some of them horse drawn, have begun to appear.

A few trams are running again, and it will not be long before the former highly efficient system will be reinstated. An extraordinarily punctual bus service is already operating in the centre, though I generally prefer to walk.

Now I am passing the perimeter of the Dead City. This is the name the locals give to the old centre, which has been almost totally obliterated. It is cordoned off and out of bounds. The destruction was so devastating here that the authorities have not attempted any restitution apart from cremating some of the corpses to stop the spread of disease, concentrating their efforts on the less heavily bombed areas. Barricades of concrete blocks, decorated with crude skull and crossbones, forbid entry under pain of death, and armed guards patrol the perimeter.

Tens of thousands of putrefying bodies still await burial within this area, and the smell of death lingers here. Its yellow, cloying, sickly odour is fainter now, but it never quite goes away. They say the decontamination teams which work in the Dead City have to use flamethrowers, not just on the decomposing corpses, but on the flies and the maggots which are so thick and bloated that boots slide and slip on them and impede access to the bodies. Huge green flies, as fat as

237

a man's thumb, are of a species never seen before. They still gorge themselves on the newly discovered bodies daily turned up by the diggers.

I have begun to shiver with the cold, although the hail has given way to light stinging rain, and I wrap my army greatcoat more tightly round myself. I pull the collar up round my neck and quicken my pace as much as my stiff leg will allow, in anticipation of a hot meal and a comfortable bed. And there's the cheering prospect of a drop of whisky tonight, I remember.

We are expected to wear uniform at all times, but like many of my colleagues in the services legal department I disobey the rule as far as possible. I've taken to stuffing my officer's peaked hat into my briefcase and pulling on a knitted cap when I walk through the city. Half bricks are all too readily at hand to tempt a starving youth to toss at a member of the occupying forces. French, American, Russian or English, we are all fair game to them. And I can't blame them.

Voices are calling out to me now through the darkness from where a fire is glowing. I stop for a moment, intrigued.

"Hey mister, got any spare change?"

"Any smokes? Beer? Candies?"

And a younger, softer voice.

"Hello, handsome! Give us a kiss then! You want some loving? A quicktime? Just five fags? Mister?"

Then a cackle of laughter from an older woman, and a glimpse in the firelight of a girl's face looking towards me, head tilted, a scarf or shawl tied round her long hair and shoulders. The other woman admonishes her.

"No good, pet! Young fellow like that don't need the likes of you. Better sticking with the married ones!"

The voices are threatening, a rumbling undercurrent of barely repressed violence. It is a chorus from some macabre production of Macbeth, with the witches huddled round their bonfire like wild beasts growling in the background, calling curses on me, the Thane, huddled in my cape after the battle. How now, you secret, black, and midnight hags! What is't you do?

A deed without a name...e'en till destruction sicken.

I shiver and move on out of hearing range of the jokes and jibes, keeping my head down and trying to ignore my wretched leg.

I'm glad to be home. By one of those unpredictable chances of war, 39 Gottfriedstrasse stands proudly unscathed by the firebombing. It is a handsome house which retains a surprising degree of its former dignity. I suppose it was built by a wealthy merchant, perhaps in the late 1800s, with no expense spared. Its finely proportioned doorway and mullion windows are miraculously intact. A smaller window is set into the mansard roof, from which can be seen a dim glow.

I walk up the worn steps to the front door, conscious of the pain in my leg. Frau Teck comes out from the kitchen as I stand in the dark hallway rubbing my hands together for warmth. She fusses nervously over me like a mother hen, helping me hang up my coat and hat and tut-tutting at how cold my hands are.

"I was worried about you, Herr Kapitän," she complains. "You are late, and there are so many bad people about these days. They are like animals in this city. Ach, it was never like this once. It was such a peaceful place once, a place to bring up children."

As far as I know Frau Teck has never had any children, but

I let it go. Against her will it seems, her eyes are drawn to my briefcase, and then away again.

"I know I'm late, but we are busier than ever in the office these days," I say soothingly, brushing the wetness off my coat. "I'm sure you must be."

"Every day more and more evil people are coming out of the woodwork. Terrible crimes were committed by just a few people."

I trot out the official line with little conviction in my voice. "Ja!" she cries. "These criminals must be found, tried, and given the same medicine that they doled out. They are fiends. Fiends! Nothing is too bad for them!" She starts to choke. "We did not know, Herr Kapitän! We had no idea. We knew there were camps – but we thought…" She grabbed my sleeve.

Here we go again, I think. I have to put up with a lot of this from local people, and am finding it increasingly hard to take. Scheiden is one of Pinkie's full-blown death camps which had 'processed' well over 200, 000 victims during the Nazi era, and it is only a few minutes' journey from this house. You must have been able to smell the smoke from the crematoria from here some days. There was talk by the Americans of marching citizens into some of these camps to see the evidence of what went on there with their own eyes, but it has already begun to seem pointless.

"Promise me you will punish them!"

I take her hand gently off my coat, swallow hard, and nod mutely. This is something else I am accustomed to. But the truth – part of the truth at any rate – is becoming clear to me. We are hell bent on prosecuting the guilty, certainly, but only the middle functionaries of the Nazi party system, the typists, clerks, managers, and low ranking officials, or even foreign soldiers conscripted into the German ranks. Meanwhile the real villains are rapidly slipping out of our reach. Argentina is said to be awash with high-ranking ex-Nazis, with more arriving by every ship and aeroplane. But a pretence of justice has to be maintained, even amongst ourselves. The work of prosecution has to be done and be seen to be done.

"Never mind that now," I say soothingly. "I have a little something for you, Frau Teck. Nothing much! But something."

Her lined blue eyes look anxiously into my face, and her bony hands grip mine..

"Some food?"

"Just some beans, a loaf of black bread, a tin of your favourite coffee and a cabbage. A little ham. Oh, and a bottle of something that calls itself whisky."

Her worn face lights up.

"Oh, Herr Kapitän, that is marvellous! And the whisky you must share with the Herr Doktor! It will do him so much good! I am so much worried about him."

"I'll go up to see him now," I say, smiling down on her. "I'll eat something later. Do you think you could find a couple of your nice glasses for me to take upstairs?"

"Of course!" she cries. "I'll bring them for you now!"

And she bustles off into her part of the house like a mouse scuttling down its hole with a stolen titbit, tail twitching with anticipation.

**Available now on Amazon or from your bookshop
ISBN 978-1-9993156-0-3**

Richard Vaughan Davies is the author of *In the Shadow of Hitler*, set in the bombed out ruins of Hamburg in 1946.

He ran a family retail business in Chester and North Wales for many years, at one time taking a three year sabbatical to read English and Italian at the University of Liverpool. He wrote a regular business column in the *Liverpool Daily Post*, and later published an advice book called *Let's Talk Shop*.

Richard retired to the Cotswolds in 2007. This was partly in order to live near Stratford-upon-Avon to indulge his love of Shakespeare, where he made the startling discoveries which resulted in him writing *In the Shadow of Shakespeare*. He has a partner Barbara and three children of whom he is also very proud, Zoe, Ric and Zanna.

Reviews are very valuable and are much appreciated.

CPSIA information can be obtained
at www.ICGtesting.com
Printed in the USA
BVHW071056290121
599084BV00006B/89